Celebrating Likes and Differences

Fun and easy theme units for exploring diversity with young children

Written and compiled by Susan Hodges
Illustrated by Janet McDonnell

Totline® Publications
A Division of Frank Schaffer Publications, Inc.
Torrance, California

Totline® Publications would like to acknowledge the following childcare professionals for contributing some of the activities in this book: Ellen Bedford, Bridgeport, CT; Nancy Nason Biddinger, Orlando, FL; Janice Bodenstedt, Jackson, MI; Marie Cecchini, Hughsonville, NY; Neoma Coale, El Dorado Springs, MO; Cindy Dingwall, Palatine, IL; Lisa Feeney, Pawling, NY; Judy Hall, Wytheville, VA; Margo S. Hunter, Westerville, OH; Bertie Kirchhofer, Chicago, IL; Paula Laughtland, Edmonds, WA; Kathy McCullough, St. Charles, IL; Susan A. Miller, Kutztown, PA; Donna Mullennix, Thousand Oaks, CA; Ann M. O'Connell, Coaldale, PA; Barbara Paxson, Champion, OH; Lois E. Putnam, Pilot Mountain, NC; Beverly Qualheim, Manitowoc, WI; Betty Silkunas, Lansdale, PA; Diane Thom, Maple Valley, WA; Margaret Timmons, Fairfield, CT; Patricia Van West, Normal, IL.

Managing Editor: Kathleen Cubley
Contributing Editors: Gayle Bittinger, Carol Gnojewski, Elizabeth McKinnon, Jean Warren
Copyeditor: Kris Fulsaas
Proofreader: Miriam Bulmer
Editorial Assistant: Durby Peterson
Graphic Designers (Interior): Sarah Ness, Gordon Frazier
Graphic Designer (Cover): Brenda Mann Harrison
Illustrator (Cover): Marion Hopping Ekberg
Illustrator (Patterns): Gary Mohrman
Production Manager: Melody Olney

ISBN: 1-57029-130-6
Library of Congress Catalog Card Number 96-60385

Printed in the United States of America
Published by Totline® Publications
Editorial Office: P.O. Box 2250
                  Everett, WA 98203
Business Office: 23740 Hawthorne Blvd.
                  Torrance, CA 90505

20 19 18 17 16 15 14 13 12 11 10 9 8 7 6 5 4 3 2 1

Introduction

Preschoolers learn through their everyday encounters. By observing and considering the similarities and differences among the things and people they know, young children can begin to understand that no two of us are the same and that differences are to be celebrated.

The 25 theme units in *Celebrating Likes and Differences* cover the topics your children know best. From babies to homes, breakfast to rice, each section brings a fresh approach to a familiar subject. The introduction to each unit gives suggestions for using everyday items and situations to explore diversity with your children. The activities that follow extend across curriculum areas, enabling your children to investigate the theme in every area of your program. Reproducible pages at the end of each section make it easy to create your own flannelboard figures, take-home books, recipe charts, and other teaching materials. Many units also include opportunities for family and community involvement.

Celebrating Likes and Differences is the perfect teaching reference for the '90s and beyond. Your children will learn to appreciate diversity while they interpret the world around them—through their own families, friends, homes, and neighborhoods.

Contents

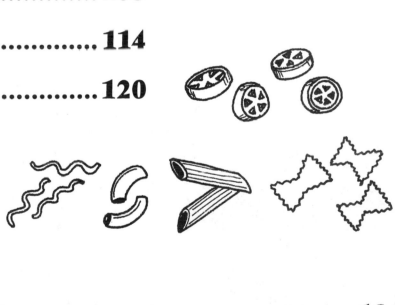

Babies

Babyhood is the most universal of experiences. We all were babies once. For preschoolers, this phase of life is a recent and fascinating one. Babyhood is a central theme in preschoolers' play, stories, and songs, as young children explore their growth and experiment with different family roles. Young children may play at being babies or at caring for them. Many preschoolers must contend with new babies in their own homes. Through When We Were Little and other activities, encourage your children to reflect on the babies they know and the babies they used to be. What similarities do babies share? How do they differ?

See how <u>Kevin</u> grows!

newborn

1 year

2 years

3 years

When We Were Little

Encourage your children's curiosity about their own history and development by helping them learn more about their babyhood. What did they look like when they were babies? What was their favorite food? Their favorite toy? Help your children understand that all people were babies once, but that not all babies look and act the same.

Ask each child's family to send in photos of the child that span a number of years. For instance, 3-year-old children might bring in photos of themselves as infants, and at 1, 2, and 3 years old. Collect the pictures and arrange them in a photo album or other display that the children can see. Give the children an opportunity to talk about their pictures. (You may wish to continue this activity over a few days.) Discuss differences and similarities among the baby pictures. Consider characteristics that change as we grow older (size, ability) and those that remain the same (gender, skin color).

Babies Everywhere

To extend your children's play and learning, provide baby-related materials in various areas of your room.

- Collect pictures of babies from greeting cards, magazines, and other sources for visual displays.

- In the home life area, set out real baby clothing, equipment, and toys as well as baby dolls, blankets, and other accessories.

- At the water table, include baby dolls, washcloths, and towels. Let the children practice bathing and drying the dolls.

- Consider adding baby dolls, small boxes, and blankets to your block area. Even children who seldom play with dolls may be inspired to build a home for the babies.

- In the art area, provide clean rags and markers. Let the children use these materials to make baby doll blankets and clothing for your home life center.

Baby Collage

Set out a selection of parenting magazines, catalogs, and other materials with pictures of babies. Let your children cut or tear out the pictures and glue them to a piece of posterboard labeled "All Kinds of Babies." Display the finished poster where everyone can enjoy it.

A Visit From a Baby

If possible, invite a baby (and his or her parent or guardian) to come for a brief visit. Encourage your children to ask questions about the baby and his or her care. Let the children help feed or care for the baby, if possible, with the parent's permission.

Whose Baby Is This?

Photocopy the patterns on pages 10–11. Color the photocopies, cover them with clear self-stick paper, and cut the patterns along the lines to make matching cards. Let your children use the cards to match the babies with their mothers.

Books to Share

The Baby's Catalogue. Janet and Allan Ahlberg. Little, Brown, 1982. Babies and their many activities are depicted in this charming picture book.

The Big Book of Beautiful Babies. David Ellwand. Dutton, 1995. From bold to bashful, bewildered to beautiful, this book is bursting with photographic first expressions that will enchant both young and old alike.

Happy Birth Day. Robie H. Harris. Illus. by Michael Emberley. Candlewick, 1996. A mother tells her child about its first day of life.

Julius, the Baby of the World. Kevin Henkes. Greenwillow, 1990. Lilly is convinced that the arrival of her new baby brother is the worst thing ever, until Cousin Garland comes to visit.

More, More, More Said the Baby. Vera B. Williams. Mulberry, 1990. Three babies are caught in the air and given loving attention by a father, a grandmother, and a mother.

A Ride on Mother's Back. Emery Bernhard. Illus. by Durga Bernhard. Harcourt, 1996. Discover how babies are carried in a variety of cultures and what they see and learn as they are carried.

Welcoming Babies. Margy Burns Knight. Tilbury House, 1994. See how each culture celebrates the beginning of life.

Baby Moves

Guide your children to imagine that they are infants. How might they move? Then lead them as they pretend to learn to roll over, crawl, and walk. Let the children take turns suggesting different baby actions for the rest of the children to perform.

Baby Snacks

Show your children an assortment of crunchy foods, such as carrot sticks and pretzels, and soft foods, such as applesauce and hot cereal. Which foods would a little baby be able to eat? Why? Which ones are only for big kids and grownups? Why? Let your children choose a soft food, such as applesauce, to eat for a snack.

Did You Ever See a Baby?

Sung to: "Did You Ever See a Lassie?"

Did you ever see a baby,
A baby, a baby,
(Rock folded arms.)
Did you ever see a baby
Wiggle her toes?
(Wiggle toes.)
Did you ever see a baby,
A baby, a baby,
(Rock folded arms.)
Did you ever see a baby
Walk on all fours?
(Crawl.)

Additional verses: Did you ever see a baby splash
in the tub (Make splashing motions); Learn how to talk
(Say "goo-goo"); Give baby a hug (Hug self).

Barbara Paxson

See the Little Baby

Sung to: "I'm a Little Teapot"

See the little baby,
Soft and sweet.
Here are his hands;
Here are his feet.
If you hug and squeeze him,
He will coo.
He loves to be so close to you!

Beverly Qualheim

New Baby

There's a new little baby at our house,
She really is quite small.
(Spread thumb and forefinger.)
I love to hold her in my arms,
(Rock folded arms.)
I just don't mind at all!

Beverly Qualheim

Mother/Baby Matching Cards

Reproducible Pattern Page, Totline® Publications, P.O. Box 2250, Everett, WA 98203

Balls

From an infant's first attempt at rolling a ball to a professional athlete's graceful maneuvers, balls are used by players of almost every age and ability. Available in an almost endless variety of materials and sizes, balls are a wonderful resource for exploring diversity with your children.

As you begin this unit, give your children opportunities to examine and play with a variety of balls both indoors and out. Encourage the children to make up their own ball games and to teach one another new ways to play. As the children share their experiences, help them notice similarities and differences among the games. If your group includes families who have lived or traveled in other countries, ask them to bring in balls or demonstrate ball games from those regions. Begin by exploring the diversity within your own group in the activity Games People Play.

Games People Play

Ask your children to name their favorite ball games. List the children's responses on a sheet of chart paper. Then read the list to your children. What sorts of games are on the list? Are there team sports such as soccer? Games such as catch? Are there any games that children have devised themselves? Why were these games chosen? Discuss the list, and help your children see that people can prefer different games, or they may enjoy the same game for different reasons. Keep the list in a place where all can see it, and add to it as you and your children learn more about balls and the games people play.

Make a Ball

Provide an assortment of materials with which your children can make their own balls. Include such items as aluminum foil, scrap paper, rubber bands, cotton, soft fabric, tape, and modeling clay. Encourage the children to experiment with the balls they have made. Which balls roll a long distance? Which ones bounce? Are some balls easier to throw? To catch?

A Brand-New Game

Older children will enjoy making up ball games of their own. To help spark your children's creativity, suggest that they begin by varying the games they already know. For instance, they might play a game of catch in which a player claps after throwing the ball, or a bowling game in which players roll a ball at a stack of blocks. If the children devise games with rules, help them record the rules on a piece of paper.

They're All Balls

Begin by gathering all the balls in your room. Look for large balls and small ones, hard ones and soft ones. If possible, include a football as well. Give your children time to investigate the balls and play with them freely. Then invite the children to sit in a circle. Place the balls in the center of the circle. Have children identify the balls as you describe them. Ask them questions such as these: "Which ball is not round? Which ball is the lightest?"

Variation: Ask the children to each bring a ball from home for this activity. Let the children tell the group about their balls and how they can play with them.

That's the Way the Ball Bounces

Photocopy the Ball Counting Cards on pages 16–17 to make one card for each of your children. Attach the photocopies to index cards, and cover them with clear self-stick paper for durability. Have each child choose a card. Tell the child to bounce and catch a rubber ball as many times as appears on the card he or she has chosen. Continue until each child has had a turn.

Extension: Let your children use the cards for counting and matching games.

Balls to Eat

Ask your children to think of different ball-shaped snacks to prepare and serve. They might choose to make popcorn balls, melon balls, meatballs, cheese balls, or other round treats.

Books to Share

Allie's Basketball Dream. Barbara E. Barber. Illus. by Darryl Ligasan. Lee & Low, 1996. Determined in her efforts to play basketball, a young African-American girl gives it one more shot with the help of a special friend.

The Ball Book. Margaret Hillert. Modern Curriculum, 1981. People play a variety of ball games on the big ball that is Earth.

The Ball Bounced. Nancy Tafuri. Greenwillow, 1989. A bouncing ball causes much excitement around the house.

Beach Ball—Left, Right. Bruce McMillan. Holiday House, 1992. This book introduces the concepts *left* and *right* as the reader follows a colorful beach ball on its airborne travels.

Irma, the Flying Bowling Ball. Tom Ross. Illus. by Rex Barron. Putnam, 1996. A black and red bowling ball named Irma dreams of flying.

Sam's Ball. Barbro Lindgren. Illus. by Eva Eriksson. Morrow, 1983. A toddler and his cat clash over who gets to play with the ball.

Stop That Ball. Mike McClintock. Illus. by Fritz Siebel. Random House, 1959. A young boy chases his ball all over town.

A Little Ball

A little ball,
   (Form circle with thumb and finger.)
A bigger ball,
   (Form circle with hands.)
A great big ball I see.
   (Form circle with arms.)
Now let's count them.
Are you ready?
One,
   (Form circle with arms.)
Two,
   (Form circle with hands.)
Three.
   (Form circle with thumb and finger.)

Adapted Traditional

Bouncing Ball

I'm bouncing, bouncing everywhere,
   (Make bouncing movements.)
I bounce and bounce into the air.
I'm bouncing, bouncing like a ball,
I bounce and bounce until I fall.
   (Drop to the floor.)

Adapted Traditional

Here Is a Ball

Here is a ball I keep on the shelf.
I can toss it and catch it
And bounce it myself.
Here is a ball that I toss to you.
Please catch it and toss it
Right back to me, too.

Adapted Traditional

Ball Counting Cards

Reproducible Pattern Page, Totline® Publications, P.O. Box 2250, Everett, WA 98203

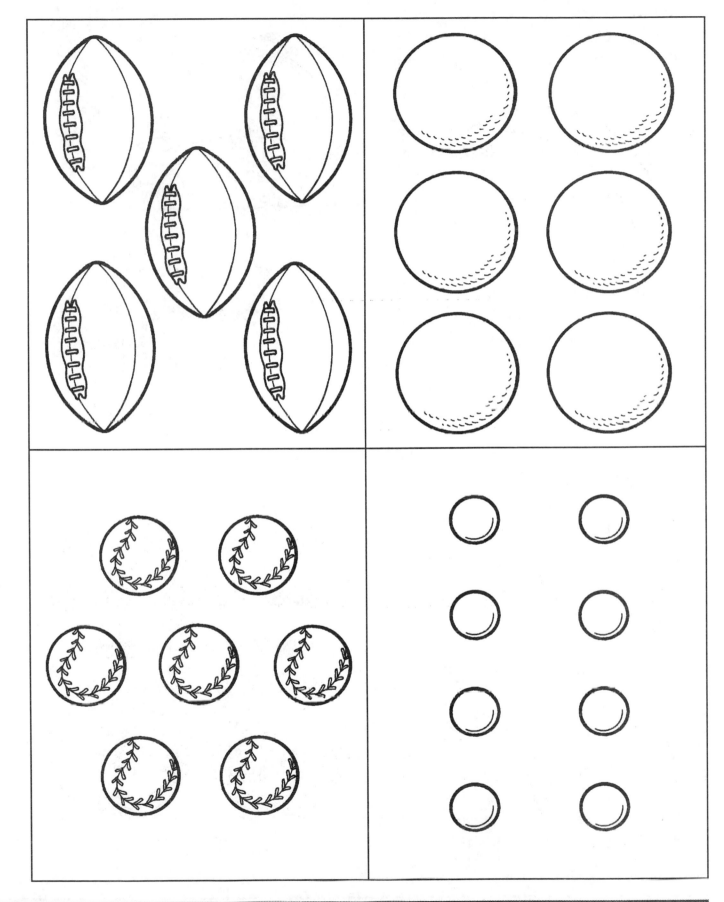

Baskets

When we think of young children and baskets, our thoughts frequently turn to springtime baskets filled with eggs, candy, or flowers. Although these are seasonal favorites, the baskets we use in day-to-day life also offer rich learning opportunities. Baskets may be functional or decorative. They can be made of straw, sticks, wire, plastic, or other materials. Baskets can hold almost anything—including babies, toys, groceries, wastepaper, or even water.

As you begin this unit with your children, invite them to bring baskets from home to explore and discuss. What are our baskets made from? When are they used? Also look for opportunities to explore how other people make and use baskets. You and your children might choose to visit the basket display at a local museum, invite a basket maker to visit, or take a trip to the basket department of an import store. The activity All Kinds of Baskets provides a hands-on introduction to a fascinating topic.

All Kinds of Baskets

Gather an assortment of baskets of different sizes, shapes, and materials. (Use baskets that your children have brought from home for a greater variety.) Arrange the baskets where your children can examine them. What might the baskets hold? Which ones are easy to carry? Which ones are best for holding big things? Little things? Set out items for the children to put and carry in the baskets. Include light, bulky materials (cotton balls or fabric scraps), delicate objects (eggshells), and grainy substances (rice).

Extension: Ask the children to sort the baskets according to size, shape (handle or no handle), or material.

Baskets Everywhere

Use baskets in the interest areas of your room to inspire and stimulate your children. Here are just a few of the ways baskets can be used.

- Store crayons, markers, and other art supplies in small baskets.

- In the block area, include baskets for storing and carrying blocks.

- In the book area, put books in some baskets, pillows in others.

- Provide a generous assortment of baskets for dramatic play in the home life area.

- Offer snack foods and napkins in baskets at snacktime.

Paper Bag Baskets

For each of your children, cut a brown paper grocery bag about 6 inches from the bottom to make a flat-bottomed bag. Set out the bags and art supplies such as paper scraps and glue, markers, crayons, or stickers. Let your children decorate their bags as they wish. Help the children attach 12-by-1½-inch paper handles to their bags.

Basket Matching

Photocopy two sets of the patterns on pages 22–23. Cut out the shapes along the solid lines and color them as desired. Cover the shapes with clear self-stick paper for durability. Mix up the shapes and let your children take turns finding the pairs of baskets that match.

Books to Share

A Birthday Basket for Tia. Pat Mora. Macmillan, 1992. With the help and interference of her cat Chica, Cecilia prepares a surprise gift for her great-aunt's 90th birthday.

Don't Count Your Chicks. Ingri and Edgar D'Aulaire. Dell, 1993. As she travels to market with a basket balanced on her head, a greedy woman dreams of the riches her eggs might bring.

Little Red Riding Hood. Trina Schart Hyman. Holiday House, 1983. On her way to deliver a basket of food to her sick grandmother, Elisabeth encounters a sly wolf.

Max's Chocolate Chicken. Rosemary Wells. Dial, 1989. When Max goes on an egg hunt with his sister Ruby, he finds everything but Easter eggs.

Mr. Rabbit and the Lovely Present. Charlotte Zolotow. Illus. by Maurice Sendak. Harper, 1962. Mr. Rabbit helps a little girl find a present for her mother's birthday.

Rechenka's Eggs. Patricia Polacco, Philomel Books, 1988. An injured goose lays 13 marvelously colored eggs in this Russian tale.

Wilfrid Gordon McDonald Partridge. Mem Fox. Illus. by Julie Vivas. Kane/Miller. 1985. A small boy tries to discover the meaning of memory to help an elderly friend.

Put All Your Eggs In One Basket

Play a counting game with your children. You will need a basket and enough plastic eggs so that each child has at least one. Have the children sit in a circle. Show them the basket and have them guess how many eggs will fit in it. Then put an egg in and say, "One." Explain that you will pass the basket around the circle. As a child gets the basket, he or she should put one egg in and then say how many eggs are in the basket. Continue passing the basket around the circle until it is full. Count the eggs with your children. Help them compare their guesses to the actual number of eggs that fit in the basket.

Little Straw Basket

Photocopy the patterns on pages 22–23 and cut out the shapes along the solid lines. Color the shapes with felt tip markers as indicated in the rhyme below and cover them with clear self-stick paper for durability. Attach a piece of hook-side Velcro or a small magnet to the back of each shape. Use the shapes on a flannelboard or a magnetboard as you read the following rhyme to your children.

Little straw basket
Colored red.
Little straw basket
To hold my bread.

Little wire basket
Colored blue.
Little wire basket
To hold my shoes.

Little plastic basket
Colored yellow.
Little plastic basket
To hold my pillows.

Little stick basket
Colored green.
Little stick basket
To hold my beans.

Jean Warren

Look Inside

Set out an assortment of baskets, each filled with a different item. Ask your children to describe each basket in turn and tell what it holds. Then sing the following song together, substituting the appropriate words for *purple* and *crayons*.

Sung to: "Did You Ever See a Lassie?"

Look inside my purple basket,
My basket, my basket.
Look inside my purple basket,
And what do you see?

My basket holds crayons;
My basket holds crayons.
Look inside my purple basket,
And that's what you'll see.

Susan Hodges

Basket Patterns

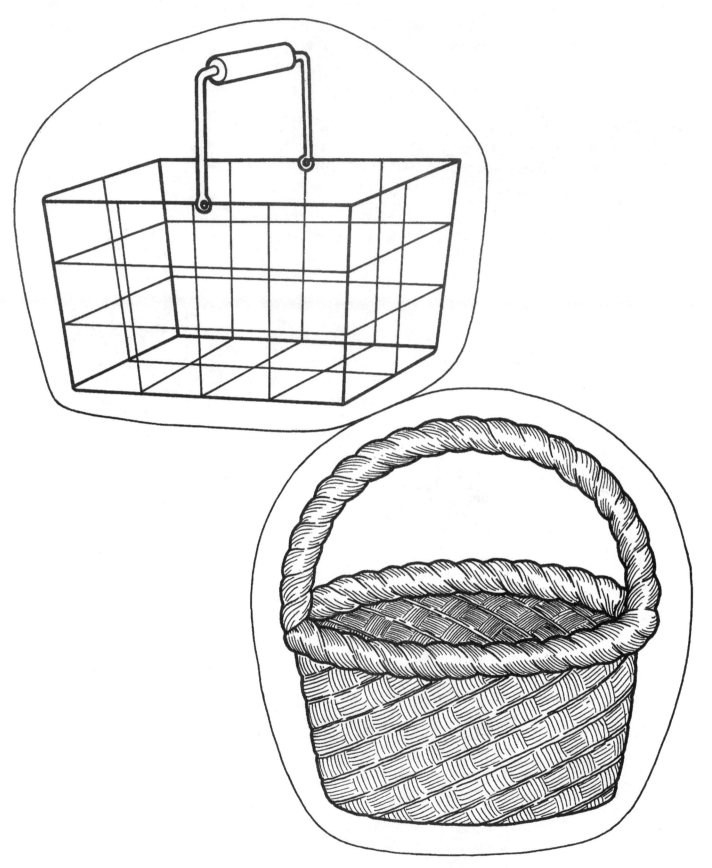

Reproducible Pattern Page, Totline® Publications, P.O. Box 2250, Everett, WA 98203

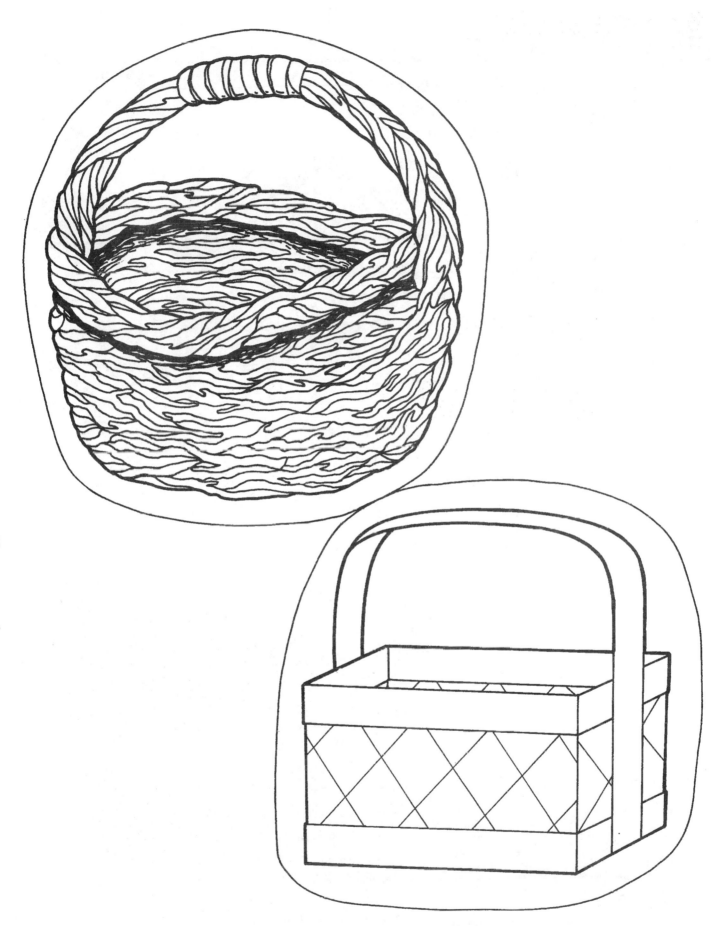

Bedtime

Because bedtime is an integral part of every child's day, it is a familiar topic for preschoolers to explore. Your children may not be aware of all the things they do to get ready for bed at night, nor may they realize that each of us gets ready for bed in our own special way. Introduce this topic by inviting your children to share their own bedtime experiences, from the hour they go to bed at night, to the type of sleepwear they prefer, to the ways that they say goodnight to their families. Let the children bring in favorite stuffed animals, blankets, or other beloved bedtime friends. Together, read books about bedtime and investigate other bedtime customs, such as the dream catcher, traditional in many Native American cultures. Explore the diverse experiences of the children in your group through the activity that follows.

Ready for Bed

Have each of your children name one thing that they do each night to get ready for bed. List these activities on a piece of chart paper. Go over the list together. Talk about each activity on the list. Who takes a bath before going to bed? Who listens to a story? Look for similarities and differences among your children's bedtime rituals, and help them to understand that we all get ready for bed, but that we have different ways of doing so.

Extension: Help older children make a bar graph of their bedtime rituals. Read the list of activities and ask the children to raise their hands every time you name one that is part of their current bedtime routine. Record the numbers and make a bar graph to show the totals.

Paper Plate Pillows

Gather a variety of stuffing materials such as wool, cotton, feathers, cornhusks, straw, rags, or paper scraps. Give each of your children two paper plates. Let them fill one paper plate (bottom side down) with the stuffing materials of their choice. Then help them tape the second paper plate (bottom side up) to the first one all around the edges. Have your children personalize their Paper Plate Pillows with crayons and markers and attach felt pieces and cotton balls to one side. Ask the children which stuffing makes the softest pillows. The lumpiest? The roundest? Talk about what kinds of pillows the children sleep on at night.

Sleep Walk

Your children will enjoy this noncompetitive version of Musical Chairs. Have each of your children bring in a pillow from home. Scatter the pillows in the center of the room, making sure that none of the pillows are touching. Take one of the pillows away. Then play or sing soothing music. Ask the children to pretend they are sleepwalking and have them circle the pillows slowly as the music plays. When the music stops, the children must find a pillow to rest their heads on. Encourage the sleepwalker without a pillow to share a pillow with someone else. Take away another pillow before starting the music again. Continue until all of the pillows are being shared.

Moon-Shaped Munchies

At snacktime, try choosing light, easy-to-prepare foods in the shape of a favorite nighttime friend, the moon. Here are just a few suggestions: round crackers topped with melted white cheese, bread rounds spread with cream cheese and grated coconut, plain mini rice cakes topped with banana rounds.

Shadowy Friends

Shadows can be scary, especially at bedtime. Help your children talk about this fear by naming objects in their rooms at home that make shadows at night. Shine a high-powered flashlight or overhead projector against a wall and show the children how to make shadows by passing their hands and bodies in front of the beam of light. Have them take turns making shadows with small, everyday items such as balls, spools, glue bottles, and rulers. Invite the children to give each shadow a funny name.

Extension: Have the children draw pictures of their shadow "friends" using black crayons or tempera paint.

Sound Maker

In fairy tales, an imaginary character called the Sandman rides the night wind to the windows of tired children and lulls them to sleep by sprinkling sand on them. Before naptime, herald the coming of the Sandman with the gentle, sleepy-time sounds made by the following simple instrument.

Find a long, sturdy cardboard tube with a lid, or close up one end of a tube with heavy paper and tape. Fill the tube one-fourth full of small, quiet-sounding materials such as cereal, rice, or sand. (Fish tank gravel works well.) Replace the lid (or close up the other end), and cover the sides with construction paper. Let your children decorate the tube with glitter, star stickers, or fabric scraps. Then show them how to shift the tube from side to side so the materials gently cascade against each other.

Books to Share

Can't You Sleep, Little Bear? Martin Waddell. Illus. by Barbara Firth. Candlewick, 1992. When bedtime comes, Little Bear is afraid of the dark until Big Bear brings him lights and love.

Goodnight Moon. Margaret Wise Brown. Illus. by Clement Hurd. Harper, 1949. In this bedtime classic, a rabbit says goodnight to the familiar things in his nest.

Hush! A Thai Lullaby. Minfong Ho. Illus. by Holly Meade. Orchard, 1996. This Thai lullaby is told in rhythmic verse with bold torn-paper illustrations. Look for the baby hiding in the pictures.

Maisy Goes to Bed. Lucy Cousins. Little, Brown, 1990. Pull the tabs and lift the flaps to help Maisy get ready for bed.

Sleep On It! Kevin Kelly and Erin Jalb. Children's Press, 1995. This informative book describes the world's beds, bedding, and sleeping customs.

Time for Bed. Mem Fox. Illus. by Jane Dyer. Harcourt, 1993. As darkness falls, parents get their children ready for sleep.

Sleepy Time Song

Sung to: "Rock-a-Bye Baby"

I put on my jammies
And wash for the night.
I jump into bed
Then out goes the light.

My mommy gives kisses
And tucks me in tight,
Then sings me a song
To last through the night.

Margo S. Hunter

Pillow Play

I love my pillow, it's soft and warm.
I hold it high, I punch it down.
I give it a poke, I give it a squeeze.
I make it bounce upon my knees.
I plump it up into a heap.
I rest my head and go to sleep.

Margo S. Hunter

Fairy-Tale Dreamer

Sung to: "Row, Row, Row Your Boat"

Sleep, sleep, go to sleep,
Daddy says to me.
I ask for a glass of milk
And a bedtime story.

When the story's through,
Daddy hugs me tight.
Then I curl up and dream
Of fairy tales all night.

Carol Gnojewski

Bedtime Everywhere Take-Home Book *by Diane Thom*

It's bedtime for the toys.

It's bedtime for the boys.

It's bedtime for the bunny.

It's bedtime for the girls.

Reproducible Pattern Page, Totline® Publications, P.O. Box 2250, Everett, WA 98203

Photocopy and cut out these pages to make take-home books for your children.

6

It's bedtime for the bear.

8

It's bedtime everywhere.

5

It's bedtime for the puppy.

7

It's bedtime for the kitty.

Reproducible Pattern Page, Totline® Publications, P.O. Box 2250, Everett, WA 98203

Bells

The sound of a bell can signal many things. At home, a doorbell notifies us when someone is at the door, an alarm clock reminds us to get up, and a kitchen timer indicates when an amount of time has elapsed. Sometimes, animals wear bells so that we can hear them approach. On the bus, a bell tells the driver to stop. In our cars, a chime may alert us that our seatbelts are unfastened. We use bells at church and at school, to make music and to celebrate special times. Bells take many shapes and forms, and make many different sounds.

Introduce your children to these and other concepts by exposing them to a variety of bells and discussing their uses. Collect bells from near and far to ring and explore together. As you examine each bell, encourage the children to think about how and why it is used. Help your children discover the many wonderful ways we use bells. And most importantly, provide ample opportunity for children to make and use bells throughout the day.

Bell Sort

Set out an assortment of bells, including such types as cowbells, jingle bells, dinner bells, birdcage bells, office bells, and hand bells. Let your children explore the bells and sort them by type, size, pitch, color, or shape. As they do so, look for similarities and differences among the bells. Which ones are usually used outdoors? Indoors? Which ones sound loud? Soft?

Extension: Ask the children to arrange the bells in a row, beginning with the largest (lowest pitch) bells and ending with the smallest (highest pitch) bells. Let the children play the bells in sequence to hear the change in tone.

Shiny Bells

Give each of your children a sheet of aluminum foil and a bell shape cut from cardboard. Have the children carefully cover their bell shapes with the foil. Attach any loose ends to the back of the bells with tape. Finish each child's bell by threading a jingle bell onto a 4-inch length of pipe cleaner, folding the pipe cleaner in half, and stapling it to the bottom of the bell for a "clapper." Let the children ring their finished bells.

Listening Match

Set out three or four different kinds of bells on a table. Place an identical set of bells behind a partition. Stand behind the partition and ring one of the bells. Ask one of your children to find the bell on the table that makes the same sound. Continue until all the bells have been matched.

Variation: Set up the bells and partition as an independent learning center for older children.

Ting, Ping, or Thud?

Suspend a wire coat hanger from a length of yarn. Invite your children to tap the edges of the hanger with various items. You might include pencils, pens, rulers, plastic spoons, metal spoons, sponges, a bar of soap, or wooden blocks. Which items allow the hanger to ring? Which make a thudding sound? Do some make no sound at all? Ask the children to sort the items according to the sound they make.

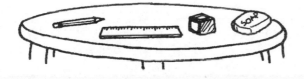

Bell Chutes

Encourage your children to experiment with pitch and tone. Provide them with a number of containers, cardboard tubes, and bells of various sizes. You might include boxes, cans, and plastic containers, and tubes from paper towels, toilet tissue, and wrapping paper. Have the children drop individual bells into a tube, then wait for the bells to tumble out of the opposite end of the tube and into a waiting container. What sounds do the balls make as they fall through the tube? As they land in the container?

Bell Count

Seat your children in a semicircle and have them hide their eyes. Ask them to count silently as you drop a few jingle bells into a container. Let them open their eyes and tell the number they counted. Empty the container and count the actual number of bells. Help the children compare this number to the number they counted. Allow individual children to take turns dropping the bells.

Books to Share

The Doorbell Rang. Pat Hutchins. Greenwillow, 1986. Each time the doorbell rings, there are more people who have come to share Ma's wonderful cookies.

Over the River and Through the Woods. Lydia Child. Illus. by John Gurney. Scholastic, 1992. An illustrated version of the well-known text describing the joys of a visit to Grandmother's house.

The Polar Express. Chris Van Allsburg. Houghton Mifflin, 1985. A magical train ride on Christmas Eve takes a boy to the North Pole, where he receives the first gift of Christmas, a bell.

The Seashore Noisy Book. Margaret Wise Brown. Illus. by Leonard Weisgard. HarperCollins, 1993. A little dog goes to the seashore and hears the sound of the sea: foghorns, the ding-dong of a bell buoy, and lapping water.

Bells Everywhere

Use the patterns on pages 34–35 to make take-home books for your children. Let the children add construction paper covers to their books. Give them real bells or paper bell shapes to attach to the covers.

My Jingle Bells

Sung to: "Jingle Bells"

Jingle bells, jingle bells,
Jingle all the way.
Oh, what fun it is to play
My jingle bells today!
Shake them fast, shake them slow,
Shake them loud and clear.
Oh, what fun it is to shake
My bells for all to hear!

Let your children shake real or pretend bells
as they sing this song with you.

Jean Warren

Bell Fingerplay

Find a mateless glove and five jingle bells. Use a hot glue gun
to glue one bell to each fingertip of the glove. (Be careful not
to get glue inside the jingle bell, or it may not ring.) Put on the
glove. Recite the following rhyme, ringing each finger's bell
as indicated.

The first little bell rang quickly.
The second little bell rang slow.
The third little bell rang loudly.
The fourth little bell rang low.
The fifth little bell rang softly.
Then all five bells rang together.
If you listen you can hear them,
Especially in winter weather.

Diane Thom

Ring Your Bells

Sung to: "Row, Row, Row Your Boat

Ring, ring, ring your bells,
Ring your bells so high.
Ring, ring, ring your bells,
Ring them to the sky.

Ring, ring, ring your bells,
Ring your bells so low.
Ring, ring, ring your bells,
Ring them soft and slow.

Susan Hodges

Bells Everywhere *by Diane Thom*

2

Bells on the hat.

4

Bells on the cat.

1

Bells on the slippers.

3

Bells on the trike.

Reproducible Pattern Page, Totline® Publications, P.O. Box 2250, Everett, WA 98203

Photocopy and cut out these pages to make take-home books for your children.

Reproducible Pattern Page, Totline® Publications, P.O. Box 2250, Everett, WA 98203

6

Bells on the bear.

8

Bells everywhere!

5

Bells on the horse.

7

Bells on the door.

Birthdays

Most children look forward to their birthdays. Use this enthusiasm to explore birthday celebrations. Share with your children the ways in which you like to celebrate your birthday. Then ask your children to describe their own family traditions. Do they like to eat favorite foods? Do special things? Guide the children in discussing the similarities and differences among their birthday rituals. Help them recognize that there are as many ways of celebrating as there are families and that every birthday celebration is special. You can extend this discussion into an ongoing project by letting your children help to plan a birthday celebration for a friend.

Older children may enjoy investigating birthday traditions from other cultures. For instance, they may be surprised to learn that in China, children celebrate their birthdays at one month, at one year, and at ten-year intervals thereafter. In Russia, birthdays are traditionally celebrated with pie.

Hint: Gather information from parents ahead of time to acquaint yourself with the different family traditions in your group.

Birthday Kit

Assemble a birthday party dramatics kit for your children to play with. Ask for their help in choosing the items to put in the kit. What items would they need in order to have a birthday party? Would they need cake? Candles? Invitations? Napkins, plates, and cups? Enlist parents' help in providing leftover materials from children's birthday celebrations. Let your children use the items in the home life center to plan a different birthday party each day. Later, discuss the parties the children planned. Point out that each was different, yet all were fun.

Hint: To make a durable birthday cake, invert a plastic whipped topping container and paint it with tempera paint mixed with a bit of liquid dishwashing detergent. Poke holes in the top with a nail and insert plastic birthday candleholders.

On Birthdays

Look for opportunities to extend the fun into all curriculum areas when your group celebrates birthdays together.

- Set out craft materials, boxes, and bows in the art area. Let the children make gifts for the birthday person.

- Use the birthday honoree's age to determine how many times you will repeat a motion during movement activities. For instance, if your classroom rabbit is 4 years old, ask the children to spin around four times and take four giant steps.

- Help your children learn a new song to honor the birthday person. Have them play their favorite instruments as accompaniment.

- Discuss the ages of the children in your group. Help your children chart each person's birth date on a calendar or a graph. (Include your own age if you dare!)

- Serve birthday treats that the children can help to prepare. Trail mix, frosted graham crackers with banana chunks, and crackers spread with soft cheese are just a few possibilities.

A Birthday Greeting

When you celebrate a birthday in your group, let your children work together to make a card for the birthday person. Gather the children around a sheet of chart paper, labeled "Happy Birthday, Kim" (substitute the name of your birthday person). Ask the children to take turns finishing the sentence, "I like Kim because. . ." Write each child's words on the chart paper. Let the children decorate the margins with rubber stamp designs or stickers, if desired. Roll up the paper, tie it with a ribbon, and present it to the birthday person.

Happy Birthday Game

This variation of Duck, Duck, Goose is fun to play at birthday parties, or anytime. Seat your children in a circle on the floor to form the outline of a cake. Select one child to be It. It walks around the outside of the circle, tapping each seated child lightly on the head and saying, "Happy, happy, happy . . . birthday! designating the child who will chase him or her around the circle and back to It's place. If It is caught, he or she becomes a "candle" and sits in the center of the cake and you select another child as It. If It is not caught, he or she selects another child as It. Once everyone has had a turn to be It, have your children count the candles on the cake.

Magnetboard Fun

Photocopy the cake and candle patterns on pages 40–41. Color the pictures as desired and cover them with clear self-stick paper. Cut them out and attach a small magnet to the back of each. Let your children use the cake and candles for counting activities.

Books to Share

Benjamin's 365 Birthdays. Judi Barrett. Illus. by Ron Barrett. Simon and Schuster, 1992. Benjamin figures out a way to celebrate his birthday 365 days of the year.

A Birthday for Frances. Russell Hoban. Illus. by Lillian Hoban. Harper, 1968. Frances is a bit jealous when her sister is the birthday girl.

Birthdays! Celebrating Life Around the World. Eve B. Feldman. BridgeWater Books, 1996. Discover how children the world over celebrate their birthdays.

Happy Birthday Moon. Frank Asch. Simon and Schuster, 1982. When a bear discovers that the moon shares his birthday, he buys the moon a beautiful hat as a present.

Hooray. A Piñata! Elisa Kleven. Dutton, 1996. It's Clara's birthday, and her party plans include having a piñata. She chooses a small, colorful dog, which she takes to heart as a real pet.

On the Day You Were Born. Debra Frasier. Harcourt, 1991. The earth celebrates the birth of a newborn baby.

Some Birthday! Patricia Polacco. Simon and Schuster, 1991. On her birthday, Dad takes a young girl to see the Monster at Clay Pit Bottom.

Birthday Party

Sung to: "The Farmer in the Dell"

Oh, welcome to our party,
We're glad you came today!
   (Beckon to birthday person.)
Won't you have a cup of tea?
It's made a special way.
   (Pretend to pour tea.)
We have some birthday treats,
We hope you'll try a few.
   (Hold out pretend plate to birthday person.)
We're so glad you came today,
Thanks for friends like you!
   (Point to birthday person.)

Jean Warren

The Birthday Child

Sung to: "The Muffin Man"

Do you know the birthday girl,
The birthday girl, the birthday girl?
Oh, yes, I know the birthday girl.
The birthday girl is Leah!
Oh, do you know how old she is,
How old she is, how old she is?
Oh, yes, I know how old she is.
The birthday girl is five.

Substitute the name and age of your birthday
child for those in the song.

Paula Laughtland

Special Day

Sung to: "London Bridge"

This is such a special day,
Special day, special day.
This is such a special day.
It's Ben's birthday.
   (Place a birthday crown on child's head.)
Today Ben is four years old,
Four years old, four years old.
Today Ben is four years old.
It's Ben's birthday!

Susan A. Miller

Birthday Cake and Candle Patterns

(See page 38 for directions.)

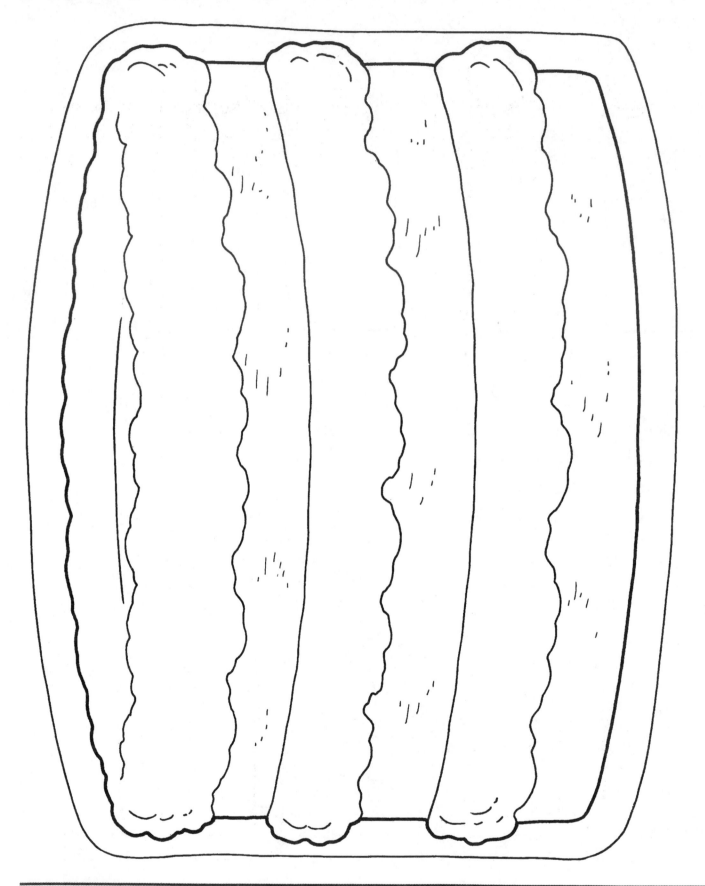

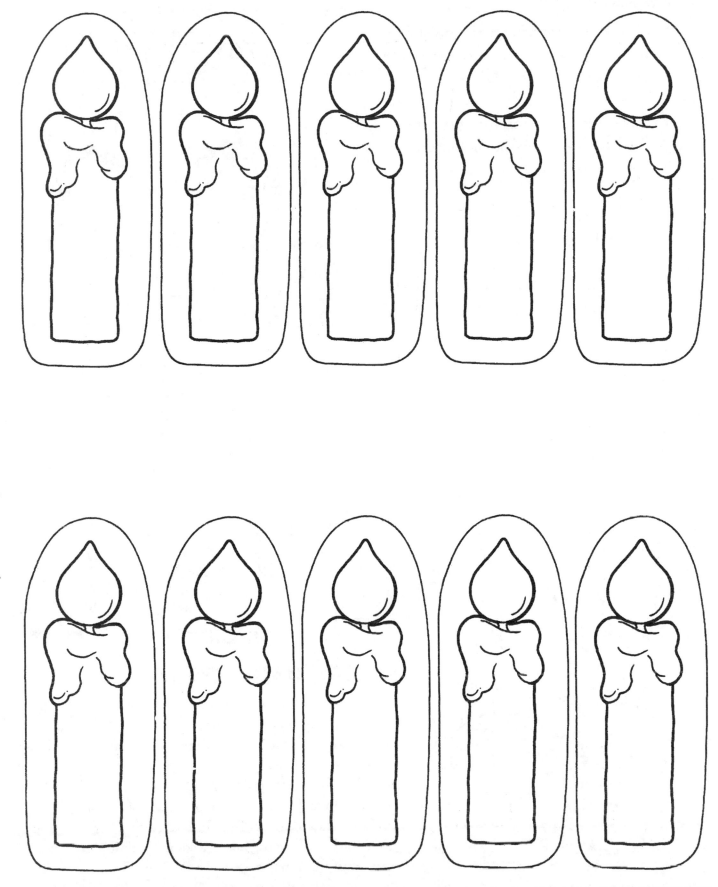

Bread

Of all foods, bread is perhaps the most common and the most versatile. We eat it daily and enjoy it in many different forms. Bread is a symbol of culture—in each region of the world, people bake bread according to custom, using the ingredients they have available. By exploring bread, your children can learn much about themselves and the world around them.

Encourage your children to talk about the bread they and their families eat at home. Together, touch, smell, and taste a few of the many varieties of bread available at your local grocery. Enjoy stories, rhymes, and songs about bread. If possible, take a trip to a bakery for a firsthand look at bakers and their work. Begin with the activity Sharing Daily Bread in order to better appreciate the similarities and differences among the breads you and your children eat.

Sharing Daily Bread

Send a note home asking that each household send in a special bread to share. In order for children to experience a variety of tastes, propose that the bread correspond in some way to their family's heritage, customs, or nationality. For example, a family might choose Italian bread, Irish soda bread, steamed buns, pita pockets, fry bread, nan, tortillas, or matzo. Each day, sit with your children and taste a different bread. Talk together about why certain breads were chosen and about differences in taste, color, texture, and shape.

Papier-Mâché Breads

Help your children tear old newspaper into 1-inch-wide strips. Then, in a large nonbreakable bowl, mix together equal amounts of all-purpose flour and water. Soak the newspaper strips in the flour mixture. Have the children wrap the papier-mâché strips around paper plates and bowls, cardboard tubes, wadded paper, or other objects to form shapes that resemble breads, such as rolls, loaves, tortillas, or slices. Let the bread shapes dry overnight or longer—a weekend is preferable. Paint the dried papier-mâché breads with white, brown, tan, and yellow tempera paints.

Baking Bread Sequence Cards

Photocopy the patterns on pages 46–47. Cut out the pictures and attach each to an index card. Cover the cards with clear self-stick paper for durability, if you wish. Let your children take turns putting the four cards in sequence.

Variation: Make more than one set of cards to use in matching games.

Our Bakery

Designate an area of your room as a make-believe bakery. Set out papier-mâché breads or other pretend breads and such cooking equipment as unbreakable mixing bowls, measuring cups, wooden spoons, and aprons. Your children will enjoy pretending to bake and sell bread in their very own bakery.

Variation: Instead of providing papier-mâché breads, set out magazine pictures of bread, paper plates, and glue. Have the children glue the pictures onto the plates to make "bread" for sale in their bakery.

Books to Share

Bread and Jam for Frances. Russell Hoban. Illus. by Lillian Hoban. HarperCollins, 1993. Frances decides she likes to eat only bread and jam at every meal until, to her surprise, her parents grant her wish.

Bread, Bread, Bread. Ann Morris. Photographs by Ken Heyman. Mulberry, 1993. Photographs reveal how people eat—and how people live—the world over.

Everybody Bakes Bread. Norah Dooley. Illus. by Peter J. Thornton. Carolrhoda, 1996. A rainy-day errand introduces Carrie to many different kinds of bread, including chapatis, challah, and pupusas. Includes recipes.

From Grain to Bread. A. Mitgutsch. Carolrhoda, 1981. This simple story traces the step-by-step process of planting wheat seeds, harvesting the crop, grinding wheat into flour, and baking bread.

The Little Red Hen. Paul Galdone. Clarion, 1973. The little red hen finds none of her lazy friends willing to help her plant, harvest, or grind wheat into flour, but all are eager to eat the bread she makes from it.

Seven Loaves of Bread. Ferida Wolff. Illus. by Katie Keller. Tambourine Books, 1993. When Milly, who does the baking on the farm, gets sick, Rose discovers that there are very good reasons for making extra loaves of bread to share with their animals and friends.

This is the Bread I Baked for Ned. C. Dragonwagon. Macmillan, 1989. Readers will enjoy chanting the repetitive phrases in this cumulative tale about preparing for a dinner party.

Quick Apple Bread

Here's a quick bread recipe your children will love to bake and eat!

- 1½ cups all-purpose flour
- 1½ cups whole-wheat flour
- ½ tsp. salt
- 1 tsp. baking soda
- ¼ cup shortening
- ½ cup granulated sugar
- 1 egg, beaten
- ¾ cup grated fresh apple
- 1 cup buttermilk

Sift flours, salt, and baking soda into a large bowl. In another bowl, cream shortening with sugar. Stir egg and grated apple into shortening mixture. Combine wet and dry ingredients in a few strokes. Briefly stir in buttermilk. Pour mixture into a greased 9-by-5-inch loaf pan. Bake at 350°F for 1¼ hours.

Hint: Remember to have your children wash their hands and be sure to sanitize surfaces before cooking and eating.

With help, children can:

- Measure and pour ingredients
- Grease loaf pan
- Pour batter into pan
- Cut cooled bread using butter or plastic knife
- Set the table and serve bread

Pound the Dough

Sung to: "Row, Row, Row Your Boat"

Push, pull, pound the dough!
Homemade bread we make.
Roll it, punch it, squeeze it, scrunch it.
In the pan it bakes.

Lisa Feeney

All Kinds of Bread

Sung to: "Twinkle, Twinkle, Little Star"

Fat bread, skinny bread, flat bread, too.
White bread, brown bread, good for you.
Toast for breakfast, a sandwich for lunch;
A roll for dinner, or a breadstick—
Crunch, crunch!
Bread is yummy, bread's a treat.
Bread is what I like to eat.

Diane Thom

Five Loaves of Bread

Cut five bread-loaf shapes out of brown felt and place them on a flannelboard. Then recite the following rhyme and have your children take turns removing the shapes. As you come to the end of each verse, pause to give the children time to name the rhyming number word.

Five loaves of bread cooling by the door,
Benji took one, now there are four.
Four loaves of bread, I hope there's one for me.
Karina took one, now there are three.
Three loaves of bread, now just a few,
Malik took one, now there are two.
Two loaves of bread, I guess I'd better run,
Molly took one, now there's only one.
One loaf of bread, will I be the lucky one?
Andy took it, now there are none!

Substitute the names of your children for those in the rhyme.

Jean Warren

Baking Bread Sequence Cards

(See page 43 for directions.)

Reproducible Pattern Page, Totline® Publications, P.O. Box 2250, Everett, WA 98203

Reproducible Pattern Page, Totline® Publications, P.O. Box 2250, Everett, WA 98203

Breakfast

Themes common to daily life help children examine and appreciate similarities and differences. Breakfast is one such theme. Almost everyone eats breakfast, yet the experience is different for each person. For instance, some people like to eat cereal for breakfast, others prefer eggs, and some enjoy grits. The foods we eat for breakfast are often reflective of our culture.

As you explore this topic with your children, look for ways to expose children to a variety of breakfast foods. Cooking magazines and women's magazines are good sources for pictures of sumptuous breakfast dishes. If your group includes families of different cultural backgounds, ask parents to send in recipes for (or samples of) breakfast foods traditional in their culture. Help your children discover that there are many ways of eating breakfast— and that all of them are delicious!

Breakfast Buffet

Ask your children to name their favorite breakfast foods. Write their responses on a chart. Then read the finished list back to them. Together, compare their responses, looking for similarities and differences. Later, let your children participate in preparing their own breakfast. If cooking facilities are available, select one or two simple breakfast dishes (such as cinnamon toast or applesauce) that the children and you can prepare. If a kitchen is not available, set out a simple buffet of breakfast cereal, sliced fruit, and milk. Give each child a bowl and let the children make their own breakfast.

Breakfast All Day Long

Introduce breakfast themes in the areas of your room.

- Include packaging from breakfast foods, cooking equipment, dishes, and other props in your dramatic play area. Your children might pretend to open a breakfast restaurant, prepare breakfast at home, or run a store that sells breakfast foods.

- Set out cereal boxes, magazine pictures, and advertisements for breakfast foods in your art area. Let your children use these materials for collages and other projects.

- Provide several different types of breakfast cereal in your snack center. Let your children use the cereal to make their own snack mix.

Breakfast Placemats

Ask your children to bring in empty boxes from their favorite cereal. Cut off and save the front panel from each cereal box. Have the children glue magazine pictures of breakfast food to the back of their panels to make breakfast collages. When the glue is dry, cover the panel with clear self-stick paper to make a reversible placemat, perfect for breakfast at home or school.

My Favorite Cup

Have each of your children bring in a favorite plastic drinking cup. Use these cups for breakfast and snack for the next week or so. Your children will enjoy using something personal from home, and you will avoid the waste and expense of using disposable cups.

Sounds Like Breakfast

Tape-record breakfast-time sounds for your children to guess. You might capture such sounds as eggs being cracked into a sizzling skillet, bacon frying, or cereal and milk being poured into a bowl.

Books to Share

The Boy Who Wouldn't Eat Breakfast. Eugene Bradley Coco. Illus. by Ann Iosa. McClanahan, 1993. Zach learns the importance of eating breakfast when he wants to play first thing in the morning. The grumbling and rumbling of his stomach lets him know he needs a nourishing morning meal.

Eat Up, Gemma. Sarah Hayes. Illus. by Jan Ormerod. Lothrop, Lee, 1988. Baby Gemma refuses to eat her breakfast until her brother gets an inspired idea.

Good Morning, Let's Eat! Karin Luisa Badt. Children's Press, 1994. Discover what people around the world eat for breakfast.

Max's Breakfast. Rosemary Wells. Dial, 1985. Max's sister tries to get him to eat his breakfast egg.

The Mother's Day Sandwich. Jillian Wynot. Illus. by Maxie Chambliss. Orchard, 1990. Ivy and Hackett's plan to give their mother a Mother's Day breakfast in bed almost turns to disaster until Mother finds a way to save the day.

Pancakes for Breakfast. Tomie De Paola. Harcourt, 1978. After the eggs are gathered, the cow milked, and the butter churned, the pancakes can be made and eaten.

Would You Spread a Turtle on Toast? Viki Woodworth. Child's World, 1992. This charming book presents the possibilities for a nutritious breakfast in rhyme.

Yum, Yum, Yum

Photocopy the patterns on pages 52–53.
Cut out the figures and color them as
desired. Cover the pieces with clear self-
stick paper and attach a piece of hook-side
Velcro or a small magnet to the back of
each. Use the pieces on a flannelboard or
a magnetboard as you share the following
poem with your children.

Pancakes, pancakes,

Yum, yum, yum.

Pancakes, pancakes,

I'd like some!

Cereal, cereal,

Yum, yum, yum.

Cereal, cereal,

I'd like some!

Additional verses: Toast, toast;
Fruit, fruit; Juice, juice; Eggs, eggs.

Jean Warren

Smells Like Breakfast

Sung to: "Frère Jacques"

Smells like breakfast,

Smells like breakfast.

Mmmm, mmmm good.

Mmmm, mmmm good.

I can smell the _____,

I can smell the _____,

Mmmm, mmmm good.

Mmmm, mmmm good.

Have your children take turns naming their
favorite breakfast smells to sing about.

Jean Warren

Breakfast Patterns

(See page 51 for directions.)

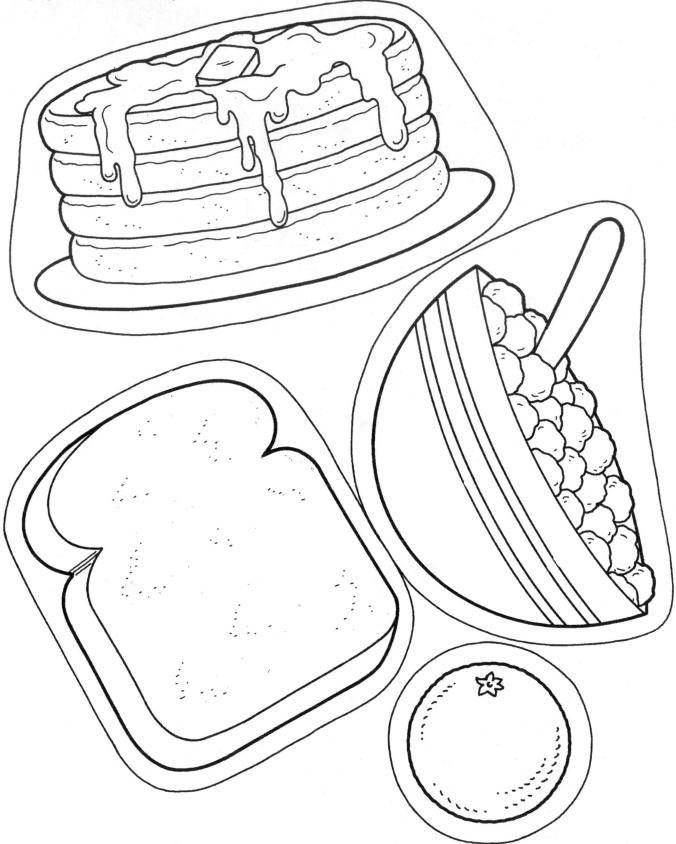

Reproducible Pattern Page, Totline® Publications, P.O. Box 2250, Everett, WA 98203

Corn

One of our most important food crops, corn is eaten by both people and animals. We enjoy corn in many different forms: cereal, baked goods, and margarine are just a few. People prepare corn in a wonderful variety of ways: they may grind it into meal to make tamales, roast it for a picnic, or pickle it for later use. Chickens, cows, and other livestock depend on corn for their daily survival.

As you explore this unit, encourage your children to share some of the ways they and their families enjoy corn. Introduce them to new ways of eating and using this versatile grain through the activities that follow.

A Cause for Celebration

Help your children discover the importance of corn in their community and around the world. If corn is grown in your area, learn what kind of corn it is, when it is planted, and when it is harvested. If possible, invite a farmer to visit your group. If your community holds a harvest celebration, look for ways your children can contribute.

You may also wish to investigate the corn festivals traditional in various cultures. For hundreds of years, the Creek, Shawnee, Seneca, and other native peoples of the Americas have sung special songs during corn planting ceremonies and performed dances to encourage rain and help the corn grow. They have also held festivals at the end of the growing season to give thanks for a bountiful harvest. Help your children plan their own corn celebration. If families in your program observe harvest or first fruits celebrations such as Succoth or Kwanzaa, invite them to share ceremonies, songs, dances, and customs with the group.

Exploring Corn

Collect an assortment of corn products for your children to investigate and compare. You might provide cornstalks, ears of sweet corn, Indian corn, feed corn, popcorn (both popped and unpopped), canned corn, corn flakes, corn chips, cornstarch, cornmeal, corn oil, or corn syrup. Then use the corn products in the various interest areas of your room to extend and inspire discovery.

- In the art area, include colorful corn kernels for collage projects.
- In the science area, let your children plant corn kernels of different varieties (popcorn, Indian corn, feed corn, etc.) in labeled cups of soil. Encourage the children to compare the growth of the various kernels.
- In the snack center, hold a corn taste test. Let the children sample freshly cooked corn on the cob, canned corn, and frozen corn.
- In the construction area, provide cornstalks and cornhusks with which the children can build shelters and crackly beds.
- In the sensory area, fill tubs with cornmeal, cornstarch, and feed corn. (Be sure to select products that have not been treated with chemicals.)

Pop-Pop-Popcorn

The experience of making popcorn engages all five senses. Bring in a hot-air popper and let your children feel some of the kernels before they are placed in the popper. For safety, have the children sit back from the hot popper while they watch as the heat changes the kernels into popcorn. They will hear the pops and smell the corn as it reacts to the heat and bursts open. Finally, they can feel the kernels in their new fluffy form as they put the popped corn into their mouth to taste.

Extension: Play lively music and let your children pretend to be popcorn kernels. Encourage them to dance and "pop" to the music.

Corn Creations

Encourage your children to investigate and discuss the various colors of kernels in ears of Indian corn. Explain how this corn got its name. Then invite them to use the corn creatively in the following activities.

CORN TOYS—Many years ago, instead of buying toys in a store, children would use dried corn to make homemade toys. In some parts of the world, children still play with corncob toys. Help your children brainstorm how to make toys using corn, felt tip markers, glue, and yarn. For example, they might use the husk for a doll's skirt, the dried silk for hair, and the cob for the body of a truck. Let your children play with their toys in the dramatic play center or the block area.

CORNCOB PRINTS—Have your children paint dried corncobs with the autumn colors of Indian corn. Let them roll the cobs on paper to create interesting, colorful designs.

CORN PENDANTS—Cut tagboard into assorted shapes and punch a hole in each with a hole punch. Set out colorful kernels of dried corn (try Indian corn or colored popcorn) and shallow containers of glue. Let each of your children select a tagboard shape, brush glue all over it, and decorate it with corn kernels to make a pendant. When the glue has dried, help the children tie long loops of yarn or string to complete their pendants.

"Corncob Print"

Carrie

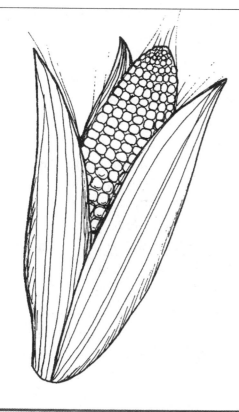

Books to Share

Corn. Ann L. Burckhardt. Capstone Press, 1966. Vivid full-color photographs help young children learn how this basic food is grown and consumed.

Corn is Maize. Aliki. HarperCollins, 1976. A simple description of how corn came to be an important food around the world.

Dragonfly's Tale. Kristina Rodanas. Clarion, 1991. After a poor harvest, two children regain the Corn Maidens' blessings for their people with the aid of a cornstalk toy, the dragonfly.

Harvest Festivals Around the World. Judith Hoffman Corwin. Messner, 1995. Learn about the special harvest festivals, customs, traditions, and planting rituals for people around the world.

Kinda Blue. Ann Grifalconi. Little, Brown, 1993. Sissy feels lonely and blue until her Uncle Dan cheers her up by explaining that everything, even corn, needs special attention every now and then.

The Popcorn Book. Tomie De Paola. Holiday House, 1978. Learn more about this favorite snack.

Raccoons and Ripe Corn. Jim Arnosky. Mulberry Books, 1987. Hungry raccoons feast at night in a field of ripe corn.

Sweet Corn

Standing in the cornfield, out in the sun,
  (Form circle with arms.)
Picking the corn ears one by one.
  (Pretend to pick corn.)
Cooking up the yellow corn, oh, what fun!
  (Pretend to drop ears into pot.)
Munching on sweet corn, yum, yum, yum!
  (Pretend to eat ear of corn.)

Jean Warren

See the Little Kernel

Sung to: "I'm a Little Teapot"

See the little kernel in the pot,
  (Crouch down.)
Turn on the heat and watch it hop.
  (Hop.)
When it gets all warmed up, it will pop.
  (Jump.)
Mmmm, it tastes good when it's hot!
  (Lick lips.)

Neoma Coale

Popcorn in the Pan

Sung to: "This Old Man"

Watch me pop in the pan,
  (Hop around.)
Try to catch me, if you can.
While I am popping to and fro,
Try to catch me as I go.

Jean Warren

Corn Everywhere   *by Susan Hodges*

2

Corn by the frog.

4

Corn by the dog.

1

Corn by the cow.

3

Corn by the chickens.

Reproducible Pattern Page, Totline® Publications, P.O. Box 2250, Everett, WA 98203

Photocopy and cut out these pages to make take-home books for your children.

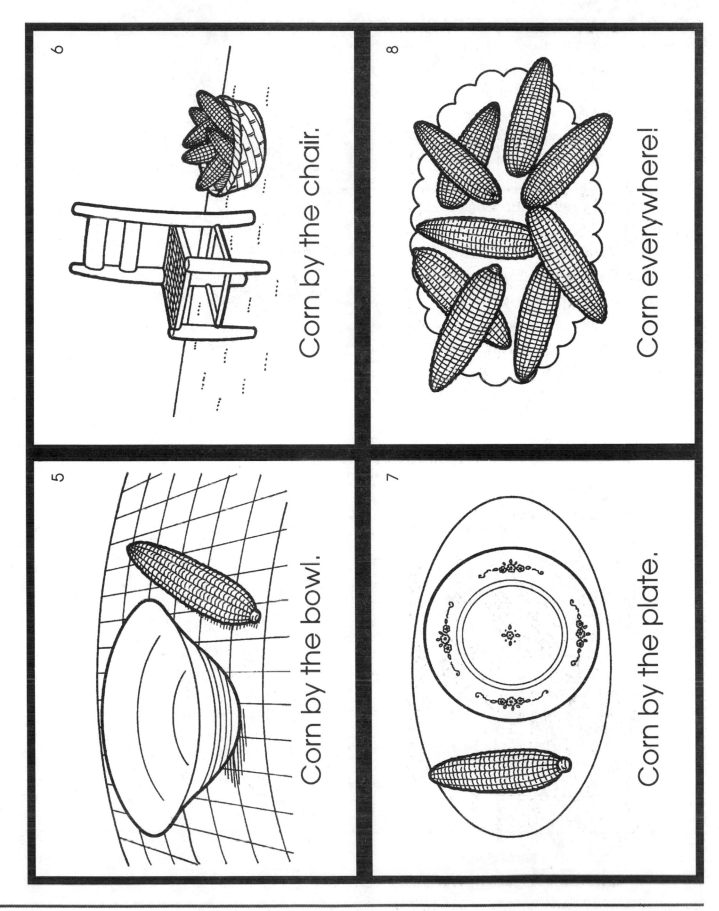

6

Corn by the chair.

8

Corn everywhere!

5

Corn by the bowl.

7

Corn by the plate.

Eggs

People enjoy eggs in an almost endless variety of ways. We may scramble eggs or fry them, poach eggs or bake them in cakes and bread. As you begin this unit with your children, ask them to tell how they like to eat eggs. Ask the parents in your program to share favorite egg recipes or to help prepare egg dishes with your group. Look for opportunities to introduce your children to some of the other ways people use eggs. You might invite someone who raises chickens to speak with your group, or include a library book on Ukrainian Easter eggs in your book area. The activities on this page are just a few of the ways you can celebrate diversity with this topic.

Scrambled eggs	
Green eggs and ham	
Fried eggs	
Hard boiled eggs	
Soft boiled	
Poached	
Omelet	

Egg Poll

Ask your children to name some of the ways that they have eaten eggs. List these on a chart. Then read off the names and have each child place a sticker on the chart to indicate the dishes they have tried. Together, analyze the results. How many children have tried scrambled eggs? Green eggs and ham? Have more children tasted fried eggs or boiled eggs? If there are any egg dishes your children would like to taste, arrange to sample these as a group.

Our Egg Cookbook

Photocopy the forms on pages 64–65 for your children. Have each child dictate how to make a favorite egg dish as you write his or her exact words on the recipe page. (Some of the recipes may be quite original.) Then let the children illustrate the recipe on the illustration page. Compile the pages into a group cookbook and photocopy the book for the children to take home to their families.

Then you mix in chocolate chips...

Watercolor Eggs

Have your children dip hard-cooked eggs in water and cover them with scraps of colorful tissue paper. Allow the eggs to dry. Remove the paper to reveal the softly colored shells.

Confetti Eggs

These festive eggs, similar to those made in some regions of Mexico, are fun to make and to break. For each of your children, tap an uncooked egg with a knife all around the shell to break off the top quarter of the eggshell. Empty and wash the shell. (Use the raw eggs for cooking projects.) Color the shells with your favorite egg dye if you wish. Allow the eggs to dry. Have your children carefully spoon a bit of confetti into each shell. Tape a piece of crepe paper over the hole in the shell. Let your children take their eggs outside and smash them. Watch the confetti fly!

Hint: Collect confetti in advance by saving small pieces of scrap paper from hole punches and craft projects.

Growing in an Egg

Help your children learn more about the many animals that come from eggs. If possible, bring in examples or pictures of eggs from different animals. To make a matching game that reinforces this concept, collect (or draw) pictures of animals that lay eggs and their offspring. Birds, turtles, crocodiles, frogs, and platypuses are just a few of the possibilities. Attach the pictures of adult animals to a piece of posterboard. Cut index cards into fourths, and attach a picture of a baby animal to each. Put each card in a separate plastic egg. Your children will enjoy opening the eggs to discover the baby animals and matching each baby to its mother.

Egg Cookery

Prepare scrambled eggs with your children. Have them observe the eggs at each step in the process. What happens when the eggs are beaten? How do the raw eggs change when they are heated?

Books to Share

The Egg. Pascale De Bourgoing. Illus. by R.M. Valat. Scholastic, 1992. Young children see a baby chick develop inside an egg, watch it peck its way out of the shell, and see it emerge into the world.

Egg. Robert Burton. Photographs by Jane Burton and Kim Taylor. Dorling Kindersley, 1994. This unique book captures the very moment of hatching in extraordinary close-up photographs.

Chickens Aren't the Only Ones. Ruth Heller. Grosset and Dunlap, 1981. Readers may be surprised at how many animals besides chickens lay eggs.

An Extraordinary Egg. Leo Lionni. Knopf, 1994. Jessica the frog befriends the animal that hatches from an egg she brought home, thinking it is a chicken.

Inside an Egg. Sylvia A. Johnson. Photographs by Kiyoshi Shimizu. Lerner, 1982. Text and photographs trace the development of a chicken egg from the time it is laid until the chick is born.

Just Plain Fancy. Patricia Polacco. Bantam, 1990. Naomi, an Amish girl whose elders have impressed upon her the importance of adhering to the simple ways of her people, is horrified when one of her hen eggs hatches into an extremely fancy bird.

The Most Wonderful Egg in the World. Helme Heine. Atheneum, 1983. The King must choose the most beautiful egg laid by three hens, one of which he will then make a princess.

Four Little Eggs

Four little eggs on the garden wall;
One leaned over and started to fall.
Down she went and broke in two.
Hurry up and get the glue!

Three little eggs on the garden wall;
One leaned over and started to fall.
Down he went and broke in two.
Hurry up and get the glue!

Two little eggs on the garden wall;
One leaned over and started to fall.
Down he went and broke in two.
Hurry up and get the glue!

One little egg on the garden wall;
She leaned over and started to fall.
Down she went and broke in two.
Hurry up and get the glue!

No little eggs on the garden wall;
No little eggs to sit up tall.
I know just what to do—
I'll hurry up and get the glue!

Jean Warren

Eggs, Eggs, Eggs

Sung to: "Three Blind Mice"

Eggs, eggs, eggs.
Eggs, eggs, eggs.
I like eggs, I like eggs.

I like them skinny, I like them wide.
I like them plain, I like them dyed.

I like them scrambled, I like them fried.
I like eggs.

Lois E. Putnam

Ruby Likes Scrambled Eggs

Sung to: "Skip to My Lou"

Ruby likes scrambled eggs, how 'bout you?
Ruby likes scrambled eggs, how 'bout you?
Ruby likes scrambled eggs, how 'bout you?
Yes, indeed, my darlin'.

Ask each child, in turn, to name his or her favorite egg dish. Then sing a new verse, substituting the child's name for Ruby, and his or her favorite egg dish for scrambled eggs.

Susan Hodges

Our Egg Cookbook

My name _____

My favorite egg dish _____

What you need _____

_____

_____

_____

How to make it _____

_____

_____

_____

_____

Reproducible Pattern Page, Totline® Publications, P.O. Box 2250, Everett, WA 98203

Our Egg Cookbook

My egg dish looks like this:

Families

The family is the center of a young child's life. Give your children an opportunity to learn more about their own families and discover a bit about those of others. Encourage the children to share stories about their families and what makes them unique. How many people are in their family? Do they have special names for their grandparents or other family members? What kinds of things do their families like to do? As you explore this topic, be sure to expose the children to books, pictures, and other materials that depict family life in all its diversity. The activity that follows is a place to start.

Meet My Family

Photocopy the forms on pages 70 and 71 for each of your children. Send the forms home along with a note requesting that each family send in a family photo. Look at the photos and read the family descriptions to your children. Let each child share a few words about his or her family. Help your children understand that families live in different ways, but that they share many of the same qualities. Later, display the photos and descriptions on the wall where your children and their families can enjoy them.

Variation: Older children will enjoy drawing pictures of their families using the form on page 71.

Family Mobile

Ask your children to draw pictures of their family on pieces of construction paper. (For younger children, provide precut paper shapes representing family members.) Help your children cut their pictures apart and punch a hole in the top of each. Let the children thread yarn through the loops of their pictures and tie them on wire hangers to make colorful mobiles.

Family Collage

From magazines or catalogs, cut out a generous supply of pictures depicting men, women, and children. Look for pictures that represent a diverse collection of individuals. Set out the pictures along with butcher paper, glue, and collage materials. (Older children can cut out the pictures themselves.) Let your children work together to make a collage of families and the things they like to do.

Hint: Family and health magazines often feature pictures of people of different ages, and sewing pattern books contain hundreds of pages of photographs of people. (Sewing shops are often willing to donate outdated pattern books.)

The Family Tree Game

Explain that families differ in many days. Some contain a few members, and some have many. Some have babies or older brothers and sisters, while others don't. Sometimes, new people, such as stepparents, stepchildren, aunts, or uncles, join families. Let your children talk about the members of their families, then teach everyone the following chant.

Thank you, thank you, thank you, tree.
Thank you for my family!
I pick you, you pick me,
I pick a _____ for my family tree.

Gather in a circle and invite one child to stand in the center. Recite the chant and have the child in the center name a family member (such as baby, grandpa, or mom) and choose a child to join the "family" in the center of the circle. Repeat the chant, letting the newest "family member" pick another child to join the circle, until everyone is in the center.

Lisa Feeney

Animal Families

Find an animal family to observe with your children. If pets or wild animals are not available, read a book or watch a video. While observing the animals, ask your children questions such as: "Do animals have families? Who are the members in their families? What do the grownups do? What do the children do?"

Also add props to your dramatic play area that might motivate children to act out animal family scenarios. For example, for dramatizing a family of birds, you might provide rags and strips of cloth for nesting materials, cotton balls and bits of yarn for food, and scarves and streamers for wings and feathers.

Books to Share

A Chair for My Mother. Vera B. Williams. Greenwillow, 1982. A child, her waitress mother, and her grandmother save dimes to buy a comfortable armchair after all their furniture is lost in a fire.

Families. Meredith Tax. Illus. by Mary Lin Hafner. Feminist Press, 1981. All kinds of families are sensitively described in this picture book.

I Meant to Tell You. James Stevenson. Greenwillow, 1996. The author remembers special times that he and his daughter shared when she was growing up.

Loving. Ann Morris. Photographs by Ken Heyman. Lothrop, 1990. Photographs capture the different ways of expressing love, with an emphasis on the relationship between parent and child.

My Mother's House, My Father's House. C.B. Christiansen. Illus. by Irene Trivas. A child describes having two different houses in which to live and what it is like to travel back and forth between them. Affirms a young child's feelings regarding a common family situation.

The Perfect Family. Nancy Carlson. Carolrhoda, 1985. An only child learns what it's like to have many brothers and sisters as she visits a neighbor for the weekend.

Snowballs. Lois Ehlert. Harcourt Brace, 1995. Some children create a family out of snow.

Through Moon and Stars and Night Skies. Ann Turner. HarperCollins, 1990. A boy who came from far away to be adopted by a couple in this country remembers how unfamiliar and frightening some of the things were in his new home, before he accepted the love he found there.

Family Times

Collect magazine pictures of families enjoying special times together. Show the pictures to your children, and invite them to discuss some of the times they have spent with their families. Then invite each of your children to draw a picture of his or her family at a special celebration, holiday, or meal. Encourage your children to tell you about their pictures. Write down their explanations and attach them to the drawings. Look at the pictures together and read each child's explanation. Discuss how families come together for many reasons—birthdays, holidays, and other special times. Help your children make a list of things that family gatherings have in common. The list might include responses such as: we celebrate with food; we are happy; we have family with us. Help your children illustrate and display their list.

Variation: For younger children, set out precut magazine pictures or paper shapes of adults and children. Let them glue the pictures to construction paper to represent their families.

All Kinds of Families

There are all kinds of families that I see,
Some are two and some are three.
   (Hold up two fingers, then three fingers.)
Some are eight and some are four,
   (Hold up eight fingers, then four fingers.)
And some are more and more and more!
   (Raise and lower all ten fingers.)

Jean Warren

Some Families

Some families are big.
Some families are small.
Some families are short.
Some families are tall.
Some families live close.
Some live far away.
But they all love each other
In their own special way.
Some families are happy.
Some families are sad.
But they still love each other,
Even when they are mad.
Some families you are born to,
Some families you are not.
But however you joined,
You are loved a whole lot!

Jean Warren

I Help My Family

I set the table—one, two, three.
   (Pretend to set table.)
That's how I help my family.
I put my toys away—one, two, three.
   (Pretend to put away toys.)
That's how I help my family.

Let your children take turns telling how they help their families, using phrases such as these: I weed the garden; I fold the laundry; I feed the puppy.

My Family

These are the people in my family:

_____

_____

_____

_____

When we're together we like to:

_____

_____

_____

_____

_____

_____

Reproducible Pattern Page, Totline® Publications, P.O. Box 2250, Everett, WA 98203

My Family's Pictures

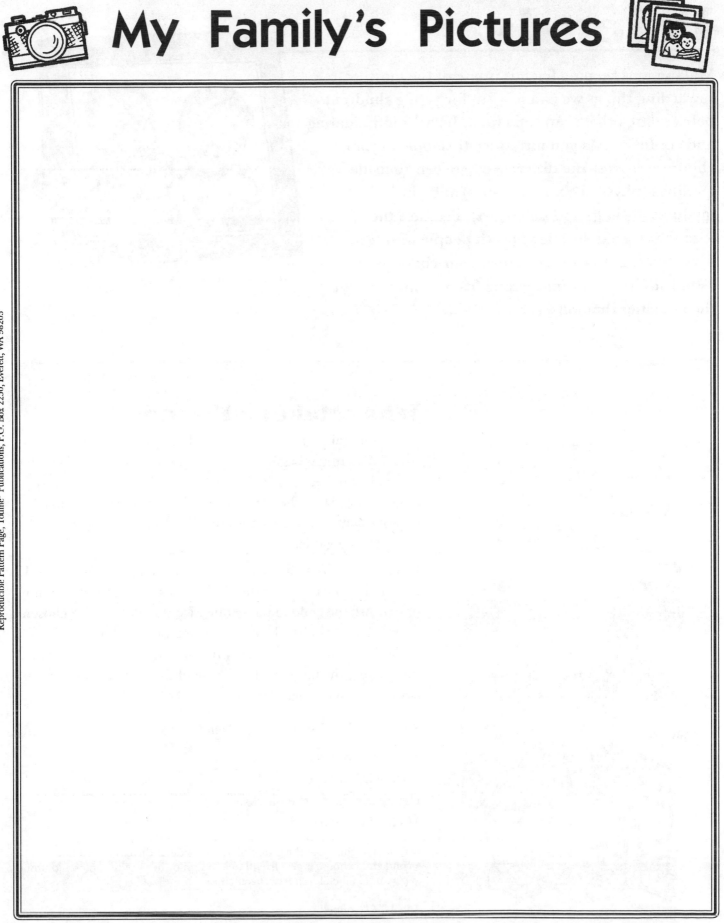

Reproducible Pattern Page, Totline® Publications, P.O. Box 2250, Everett, WA 98203

Friends

Making and keeping friends is one of the most rewarding things we can do. But for young children, befriending others can sometimes be a bit intimidating and confusing. As you introduce this topic to your children, discuss the difference between "outside" qualities (physical characteristics) and "inside" qualities (feelings and behaviors). Promote the idea that we can be friends with people who seem very different from us. Support your children in establishing and strengthening friendships through the activities that follow.

What Makes a Friend?

Julie is my friend. She always makes me laugh.

With your children, discuss the qualities that make a good friend. You might begin by asking questions such as, "Who has a friend who likes to share? Does anyone have a friend who hugs them?" Help the children decide on some words that describe someone who is a friend. Then invite them to play the following game.

Have the children form a circle with one child in the center. Let the child in the center of the circle choose a friend to join him or her. Ask the child to name one nice thing about the chosen friend. Then join hands with the remaining children and circle around the pair in the center while singing the following song, substituting the name and attribute of the child in your group for those in the song.

Sung to: "The Farmer in the Dell"

Michael is my friend.
Michael is my friend.
He always shares the blocks with me.
Michael is my friend.

Let the first child join the group on the outside of the circle and have the second child choose a new friend to join him or her in the center. Continue to play until all children have been chosen.

Ann M. O'Connell

Friendship Pillow

Ask your children how they know when people are friends. Maybe they see people smile at each other, hug, play together, talk, kiss, or hold hands. Tell them that they will have a chance to show everyone they are friends by making hand-holding pillows. Cover the floor with plastic or another protective covering and set out several shallow containers of flesh-toned nontoxic fabric paint. (Be sure to provide colors of paint that represent the skin tones of the children in your group.) Set out several light-colored pillowcases. Invite your children to cooperate as they dip their hands in the paint and print adjoining handprints on the pillowcase. Allow the pillowcase to dry, then fill it with a pillow. These Friendship Pillows make a nice addition to your reading area.

Reading Corner

We Are Friends

Talk with your children about how all people have things in common, yet each of us is unique. We all have bodies, but some of us are boys, and some are girls; some are big, and some are small. We all have families, but some of us have moms, some have dads, and some have moms and dads. Friends, too, are similar in some ways and distinct in others.

Label a large piece of paper "We Are Friends." Have your children cut or tear out pictures of children from old magazines or catalogs. Let them attach the pictures to a large piece of butcher paper to make a visual display of friends.

Friendly Puppets

Enable your children to act out friendly behaviors with these lifelike puppets. Collect a photograph of each child. Cut the figures from the photos and attach each to the end of a craft stick to make a stick puppet. Create a theater for the puppets by covering a shoebox with colorful paper. Cut ½ inch slits in the bottom of the box, then turn the box upside down and place the sticks in the slits to hold the puppets.

Books to Share

I Have a New Friend. Kathleen Allan-Meyer. Photographs by Mike Spinelli. Barrons, 1995. Lisa writes a letter to her grandmother telling all about her new Japanese friend at nursery school.

Jamaica's Find. Juanita Havill. Illus. by Anne Sibley O'Brien. Houghton Mifflin, 1986. Jamaica and Kristin become friends when Jamaica finds a stuffed dog in the park.

Jessica. Kevin Henkes. Greenwillow, 1989. Ruthie does everything with her imaginary friend Jessica, and then on her first day at kindergarten, she meets a real new friend with the same name.

Matthew and Tilly. Rebecca C. Jones. Illus. by Beth Peck. Dutton, 1991. Set in the diverse neighborhood of a big city, this poignant and universal story of friendship tells about two best pals who share everything together, even making up after a quarrel.

The Rainbow Fish. Marcus Pfister. North-South Books, 1992. The vain Rainbow Fish learns the importance of sharing and friendship. Shimmering illustrations make this award-winning book a treat.

We Are Best Friends. Aliki. Mulberry Books, 1982. When Robert's best friend Peter moves away, both are unhappy, but they learn that they can make new friends and still remain best friends.

Wiggly Friends

4 envelopes plain gelatin

4 cups apple juice, divided

Raisins, shredded coconut, or other decoration

Let your children help you pour the gelatin powder into a large bowl. Pour 1 cup of cold apple juice on top of the gelatin, and let stand 1 minute. Heat the remaining 3 cups of apple juice to boiling, and stir the hot juice into the gelatin mixture. Pour the gelatin mixture into a 9-by-13-inch pan sprayed with nonstick cooking spray, and chill at least 3 hours or until gelatin is firm.

Spray child-shaped cookie cutters with nonstick cooking spray and help each child cut two figures from the hardened gelatin. Encourage each child to cut out one Wiggly Friend for him or herself and one to share with a friend. Have your children add facial features to their Wiggly Friends with ingredients such as raisins, shredded coconut, and cereal.

Have your children share their Wiggly Friends with one another. Discuss how friends share things. Sometimes friends share their food. Ask your children to name other things friends share.

A Friend Is Someone Special

A friend is someone special,
And do you know why?
A friend is someone special
On whom you can rely.
A friend will listen to you,
And help you when she can.
A friend is kind and caring,
And always your biggest fan.
So when you find somebody
On whom you can depend,
You know at last that you
Have found yourself a friend.

Jean Warren

A Friend We Like

Sung to: "She'll Be Coming Round the Mountain"

Oh, I know a friend we all like very much.
Oh, I know a friend we all like very much.
Oh, I know a friend we all like,
Oh, I know a friend we all like,
Oh, I know a friend we all like very much:
Claire!

Substitute the name of one of your children for *Claire*.

Lois E. Putnam

Making Friends

Sung to: "Yankee Doodle"

Making friends and keeping them,
You learn to help another.
Just keep in mind the best thing is
To always love each other.
Hug your neighbor next to you,
Shake another's hand.
If you're kind in all you do,
You'll always have a friend.

Judy Hall

Friendship Book

Help your children make a group book that celebrates friendship. Photocopy the pattern on the facing page for each child in your group. Ask each child to complete the phrase "I like it when my friend . . . ." Write the children's responses on their pages. Provide drawing supplies with which the children can illustrate or decorate their pages. Compile the finished pages into a book, adding a durable cover. Keep the book in your reading area, where all can enjoy it.

Reproducible Pattern Page, Totline® Publications, P.O. Box 2250, Everett, WA 98203

My name _____

I like it when my friend _____

Getting to School

By exploring the ways they and others arrive at school, your children can begin to appreciate the diversity that surrounds them. Invite your children to share how they arrived at school. As the children discuss their travel experiences, encourage them to look for similarities and differences. Do some children come with their fathers? With their grandmothers? Does anyone ride on a bus? Walk?

Ask your children to imagine that they no longer have their usual way of getting to school. What alternative ways can they devise? Help the children understand that we all get to school, but that each of us comes in a slightly different way. Then use the following activity to make this topic a family affair.

Family Interview

Invite your children's relatives to share their memories of traveling to school. Photocopy pages 82 and 83 to make interview forms for the children to take home. Have each child give the form to a parent, a grandparent, or an older sibling to fill out. When the children return the completed forms, read the responses aloud to the group.

Interview
Form
Name of relative: Grandpa Dan
How did you get to school when you were young?
When I was a little boy we lived on a farm. My brother, your great-uncle Al, and I used to ride to school on a white horse named Clancy. My brother rode in front, and I sat behind and held on tight.

See Us Go

Collect a photograph of each of your children. Photocopy these pictures. Set out precut paper vehicle shapes. Have your children glue a copy of their picture to a shape that represents how they go to school. If some of your children walk to school, have them glue their picture to an outline of an adult and a child walking.

Our Magic Ride

Clear an area of your room and set out several chairs. Have your children arrange the chairs to make a make-believe bus, a car, or a boat, assisting them as necessary. Provide a clean cardboard pizza wheel for a steering wheel. Encourage the children to make and sell tickets for their ride. Let them bring stuffed animals, dolls, or other passengers along on their trip.

A Traveling Tale

In a pillowcase or other opaque bag, gather several toys that represent different modes of transportation, such as a car, a bus, a boat, an airplane, and a horse. Tell your children a story about a character who wants to go to school. Suggest ways the character might get there, giving hints about the toys in the bag. Have your children name a form of transportation, then take the corresponding toy out of the bag. Continue until the bag is empty.

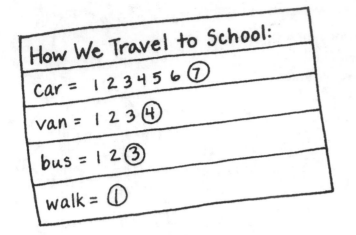

How We Travel to School:

car = 1 2 3 4 5 6 ⑦

van = 1 2 3 ④

bus = 1 2 ③

walk = ①

Ways We Go

Make a chart listing the various ways your children travel to school, as shown in the illustration. Show the chart to your children. As you read each heading, have the children raise their hands to indicate how they traveled to school. Count the responses and tally them in the appropriate column. Then, with your children's help, count the responses in each column. What is the most frequent way that children come to school? The least frequent?

Books to Share

Arthur's Back To School Day. Lillian Hoban. HarperCollins, 1996. While hurrying to get on the school bus, Arthur and his friend unknowingly switch their lunch boxes.

My First Day at School. Ronnie Sellers. Illus. by Patti Stren. Caedmon, 1985. Ben experiences his first day at school and finds it an exciting place to learn and have fun.

School. Emily Arnold McCully. Harper Trophy, 1987. In this wordless picture book, a too-small mouse follows his siblings to school.

School Days. B. Hennessy. Illus. by Tracey Campbell Person. Viking, 1990. Young children will relate well to this simple, rhyming text that tells about a day at school.

The Secret Shortcut. Mark Teague. Scholastic, 1996. Because Wendell and Floyd have trouble getting to school on time, they decide to take a shortcut, which leads to an unexpected adventure.

Starting School. Allan and Janet Ahlberg. Puffin, 1990. This book shows children what going to school is all about.

This Is the Way We Go to School. Edith Baer. Illus. Steve Bjorkman. Scholastic, 1990. Young readers are taken on a journey around the world, celebrating the many different ways children travel to the classroom.

The Trek. Ann Jonas. Greenwillow Books, 1985. A child describes her trip through a jungle and across a desert on the way to school.

Getting There

Have your children spread out in an open area. Then ask them to imagine that they are traveling to school. How will they go? Will they walk? Skip? Hop? Travel by boat, airplane, or truck? Ask your children to think of new ways to travel, then have them act out each one.

Ready, Set, Go!

Share the following open-ended poem with your children. Ask the children to suggest words to fill in the blanks. Reread the poem with your children's suggestions.

Ready, set, go!
We're on our way.
But how should we get
To school today?
We could ride a _____
All the way,
Or we could take a _____
To school today.

We could ride our _____
All the way,
Or we could take a _____
To school today.
Ready, set, go!
We're on our way.
That's how we'll get
To school today!

Jean Warren

We're Going Off to School

Sung to: "The Farmer in the Dell"

We're going off to school,
We're going off to school.
Come with us–we'll ride the bus.
We're going off to school!

We're going off to school,
We're going off to school.
It's rather far–we'll take the car.
We're going off to school!

We're going off to school,
We're going off to school.
We like to walk along and talk.
We're going off to school!

Have the children stand as they sing the verse that describes how they arrived at school.

Nancy Nason Biddinger

Interview Form

name of relative —————————————————————

How did you get to school when you were young?

_____

_____

_____

_____

_____

_____

_____

_____

_____

_____

Reproducible Pattern Page, Totline® Publications, P.O. Box 2250, Everett, WA 98203

Interview Form

name of relative —————————————————————————

How did you get to school when you were young?

_____

_____

_____

_____

_____

_____

_____

_____

_____

_____

_____

Reproducible Pattern Page, Tidline® Publications, P.O. Box 2250, Everett, WA 98203

Grandparents

Most children enjoy a special relationship with their grandparents. Help your children discover that grandparents may live nearby or far away; they may live with us or have homes of their own. Grandparents come in different shapes and sizes, but seem to share one thing: love. As you explore this topic with your group, look for ways to include the grandparents who live nearby. You might invite local grandparents to come in and help with a cooking activity, read the children a story, or accompany your group on a walk. If convenient, let your children plan a special celebration for their grandparents (and honorary grandparents). Begin by exploring through the following activity the things that make grandparents special.

Special Because . . .

Invite your children to talk about grandparents and the reasons they are special. Encourage the children to tell about their own grandparents. Label a piece of paper "Grandparents Are Special Because . . ." and list the children's ideas on the chart. Give the children time to draw pictures of their grandparents and the things they like to do together. Display the chart and pictures where all can enjoy them. (For younger children, provide precut magazine pictures of older people with young children. Have the children glue these pictures to the chart.)

Variation: Have the children draw things they like to do with their grandparents. Invite the children to dictate sentences about their pictures. Compile the pages into a group book. Make copies of the book for your children to take home.

Going Visiting

Let your children share memories of visits to their grandparents. Do their grandparents live nearby or far away? Did the children ride in a car to get there? Did anyone take a plane? What did they do when they visited? Then let the children act out a visit to their grandparents' house. How will they get there? What will they do?

Adopt a Grandparent

Contact a local retirement center, and arrange for a few of the residents to visit your group. Seniors enjoy the interaction with young children, and children take pride in showing visitors around. Continue this special partnership throughout the year by inviting the seniors to holiday performances or taking your children to visit them at their center.

Meet Our Grandparents

Photocopy the form on page 88 for your children. Let each child take a form home and bring it back along with a photo of his or grandparents. Read the pages aloud to the group, and display the pictures and forms where everyone can see them.

Extension: Older children may enjoy using the form on page 89 to draw portraits of their grandparents.

Meet My Grandparents

My name: Katie Smith
My Grandparents are: Doris and Sam Smith
I call them: Nana and Bompie
They live in: Chicago
When we're together we: read books, make cookies, watch movies

Books to Share

Introduce your children to these and other books that show the many roles that grandparents play in children's lives.

Abuela. Arthur Dorros. Illus. by Elisa Kieven. Dutton, 1991. While riding on a bus with her grandmother, a young Hispanic girl imagines that they are carried up into the sky and fly over the sights of New York City.

The Best Present. Holly Keller. Greenwillow, 1989. When Rosie is unable to visit her grandmother in the hospital, she sends her a special present instead.

Grandpa's Face. Eloise Greenfield. Illus. by Floyd Cooper. Putnam and Grosset, 1988. Seeing her beloved grandfather making a mean face while he rehearses for one of his plays, Tamika becomes afraid that someday she will lose his love and he will make a mean face at her.

Homeplace. Anne Shelby. Illus. by Wendy Anderson Halperin. Orchard Books, 1995. A grandmother and grandchild trace their family history.

I Dance in My Red Pajamas. E.T. Hurd. Illus. by Emily Arnold McCully. Harper, 1982. This delightful picture book captures the special relationship between a child and her grandparents.

Not So Fast, Songololo. Niki Daly. Puffin, 1987. In South Africa, Malusi goes shopping with his granny, Gogo, and is delighted when he gets a pair of new red shoes.

Robert Lives with his Grandparents. Martha Whitmore Hickman. Illus. by Tim Hinton. A. Whitman, 1995. Robert is embarrassed to admit to his classmates that he has lived with his grandparents since his parents' divorce.

Tom. Tomie De Paola. Putnam, 1993. Aside from having the same name, Tommy and his grandfather Tom share a sense of humor.

Grandma's Coming

Sung to: "She'll Be Coming Round the Mountain"

Grandma's coming soon to visit, yes, she is.

Grandma's coming soon to visit, yes, she is.

Grandma's coming soon to visit,

Yes, she's coming soon to visit,

Grandma's coming soon to visit, yes, she is.

Additional verses: "She'll be driving a new car when she comes; She'll be flying on an airplane when she comes; Oh, we'll be so glad to see her when she comes." Repeat the song, substituting *Grandpa* or a visitor's name for *Grandma*.

Jean Warren

I Love Grandma

Sung to: "Frère Jacques"

I love Grandma,

I love Grandma.

Yes, I do.

Yes, I do.

She takes me to the playground,

She takes me to the playground.

She loves me too.

She loves me too.

I love Grandpa,

I love Grandpa.

Yes, I do.

Yes, I do.

He makes my breakfast,

He makes my breakfast.

He loves me too.

He loves me too.

Ask your children to suggest other things that grandmas and grandpas do. Sing the song again, substituting these phrases for *she takes me to the playground* and *he makes my breakfast*.

Jean Warren

Grandma and Grandpa

Grandpa is my buddy,

Grandma is too.

They always try to help me

With what I want to do.

They help me learn to hammer,
  (Pretend to pound nails.)

They help me learn to sew.
  (Pretend to sew with needle.)

They help me learn to play games,
  (Pretend to play cards.)

And make my modeling dough.
  (Pretend to knead dough.)

They always take the time

To explain how things go.

They always take the time

To explain how things grow.

Grandpa is my buddy,

Grandma is too.

They always try to help me

With what I want to do.

Jean Warren

Meet My Grandparents

My name:_____

My Grandparents' names are: _____

_____

I call them: _____

_____

They're the parents of: _____

_____

They live in: _____

When we're together, we: _____

_____

_____

_____

_____

_____

_____

Reproducible Pattern Page, Totline® Publications, P.O. Box 2250, Everett, WA 98203

My Grandparents

Hats

In color, size, shape, and function, hats are as diverse as the children in your group. And while they are a part of everyone's experience, we all use hats in different ways. Hats can protect us from the weather or from personal injury. Some hats are worn at special times such as weddings or holidays. Others are part of a uniform for work, school, or team activities.

As you explore this topic, help your children discover some of the ways hats are worn in their community and beyond. Encourage the children to bring in their favorite hats from home and talk about what makes each hat special. You might invite community helpers who wear hats in the workplace, such as firefighters, cooks, or construction workers, to talk about how their hats assist them in their work. Also collect pictures of people from different cultures wearing hats. You can use these in visual displays, or your children can use them to make a group collage. Activities such as Hat Dance and Hat Sort provide an enjoyable introduction to the world of hats.

Hat Dance

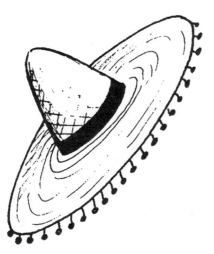

Some hats have special uses that set them apart from everyday hats. And some everyday hats have a tradition of being used in surprising ways. Mexican hats called *sombreros* are everyday, wide-brimmed hats used for protection from the sun. However, during celebrations, sombreros are used as props for a hat dance. Place a hat on the floor in front of each of your children and put on some lively music. Let your children dance around their hats.

Extension: Talk about other special uses for hats. Examples include women carrying food and laundry on top of their hats, pioneers scooping water out of streams with their hats, miners using their hats with lamps to see in mines, and astronauts using their special hats with oxygen to help them breathe in space.

Hat Sort

Invite your children to bring in a variety of hats from home. Examine the hats with your children and discuss how they are all alike and different. Have them guess who they might be, where they might go, and what they might do if they were wearing each hat. Put all of the hats in a large box, and let your children take turns sorting them into three piles, one for hats worn to protect us from weather, one for sports hats, and one for decorative hats.

Pass the Hat

Make a creation station at a long table by setting out decorating materials such as tissue paper, ribbon, glitter, buttons, feathers, and fabric scraps. Start creating a hat at one end of the table by instructing the first child to glue one decoration to the bottom side of a sturdy paper plate. When the first child is finished, ask him or her to pass the plate down the table. Let each of your children have at least one turn decorating. Complete the paper plate hat by stapling two 12-inch pieces of ribbon to opposite sides so that the hat can be tied under the chin like a bonnet.

Silly Hat Box

Collect several nonaluminum metal colanders, shoelaces, pipe cleaners, and magnets. Place the items in a box. Let two or three children at a time use these items to make Silly Hats. Show them how to thread the shoelaces and pipe cleaners through the holes in the colanders. Let them arrange magnets on the colanders as desired. Have the children model their creations.

Extension: Take photos of your children wearing their Silly Hats and decorate the box with the photos.

Toss the Hat

Find a sturdy coat stand with hooks and place it in the center of your room. Set out several old hats. Show your children how to hang the hats on the hooks, and let them practice this process. Encourage older children to figure out ways to place hats on the highest hooks, such as using stepladders or the ends of broomsticks. Then have the children toss the hats at the coat stand to make them hang from the hooks. Applaud all hat tossing attempts.

Books to Share

Aunt Flossie's Hats (And Crab Cakes Later). Elizabeth Fitzgerald Howard. Illus. by James Ransome. Clarion, 1990. Sara and Susan share tea, cookies, crab cakes, and stories about hats when they visit their favorite relative, Aunt Flossie.

Hats, Hats, Hats. Ann Morris. Photographs by Ken Heyman. Lothrop, Lee, 1989. Photographs show how people wear and use hats in many regions of the world.

Hats Off to Hats! Sara Corbett. Children's Press, 1995. Explores the world of hats, discussing the origin and function of different kinds found around the world.

Jennie's Hat. Ezra Jack Keats. HarperCollins, 1966. Jennie's friends, the birds, turn her drab hat into a beautiful one.

Martin's Hats. Joan W. Blos. Illus. by Marc Simont. Morrow, 1984. A variety of hats afford Martin many adventures.

Whose Hat? Margaret Miller. Greenwillow, 1988. Presents color photographs of hats that represent various occupations.

Whose Hat Is That? Ron Roy. Houghton Mifflin, 1990. Colorful photographs present 18 different types of hats.

Whose Hat Was That? Brian Wildsmith and Rebecca Wildsmith. Harcourt Brace, 1993. The wind blows hats from people's heads onto animals in different places throughout the world, eventually blowing all of the hats to the moon.

Eat Your Hat

This quick and tasty snack gives new meaning to the old expression "I'll eat my hat." Give each child a square slice of cheese and half of a hot dog bun. Demonstrate how to make a hat by placing the bun on a plate and topping it with a piece of cheese. Let your children fill their brims with egg, tuna, ham or chicken salad. Set out condiments such as catsup and mustard in squeeze bottles, olives, pickle rounds, and julienned carrot strips. Your children will have fun personalizing and eating their own hat sandwich creations.

A Year of Hats

Tyler has a hat that's furry and tight
For January's frosty nights.
Jessica has a hat with hearts and bows
To wear in February's snows.
Annie has a hat with tassels long
When the cold March winds blow strong.

James has a hat to keep him dry
As April's showers fill the sky.
Emily has a hat with flower sprays
To wear outdoors during May.
Maria has a hat with a brim so wide
To wear in June when she's outside.

Lee has a hat for beachtime fun
In hot July's sand and sun.
Marcus has a hat to shade his eyes
From the sunny August skies.
Sam has a hat to wear to school
When mild September days grow cool.

Mia has a hat for trick or treat
In October down her street.
Josh has a hat of colored wool
When November days are cool.
Libby has a hat to keep her warm
From cold December's wintry storms.

Substitute the names of your children
for those in the poem.

Lois E. Putnam

I've Seen a Hat

*Sung to: "The Bear Went Over
the Mountain"*

I've seen a hat on a scarecrow.
I've seen a hat on a snowman.
I've seen a hat on a lady,
While she was sipping tea.

I've seen a hat on a cowboy,
I've seen a hat on a farmer,
I've seen a hat on a baker
Who baked me fresh cookies.

But if I look into the mirror,
If I look into the mirror,
If I look into the mirror,
I see a hat on me.

I see a hat on me,
I see a hat on me.
When I look into the mirror,
I see a hat on me.

Diane Thom

2

Hats on firefighters, shiny and new.

4

Hats on astronauts when they land.

1

Hats on police officers, starchy and blue.

3

Hats on marchers in a band.

Reproducible Pattern Page, Totline® Publications, P.O. Box 2250, Everett, WA 98203

Photocopy and cut out these pages to make take-home books for your children.

Reproducible Pattern Page, Totline® Publications, P.O. Box 2250, Everett, WA 98203

6

Hats on artists when they draw.

8

Hats on almost everyone!

5

Hats on farmers, made of straw.

7

Hats on babies out in the sun.

Homes

Whether it is a mobile home in a park or a condominium in a city, most children have a home they can call their own. Help your children understand the diversity and uniqueness of all homes by discussing the characteristics of their own homes. What do they look like? What building materials were used? Who lives in them? How are their homes similar? How are they unique?

Support your children as they investigate the homes in their community and beyond. You might take the children on a drive to look at neighborhood homes, read them books about homes in distant towns, or display pictures of a variety of homes in the block area to inspire young builders. The following activity enables your children to learn more about themselves and the others in your group.

My Home Is . . . .

Hang a sheet of chart paper at your children's eye level. At the top write "My home is . . . ." Read the words aloud and ask each child to finish the sentence with his or her own words. Write each child's sentence on the chart. Let the children attach photographs or drawings of their homes around the border. Display the chart for everyone to see. As you look at the finished display with your children, help them understand that people live in many different kinds of homes.

Extension: Older children might enjoy adding a creative visualization dimension to this activity. Ask 4- or 5-year-olds to close their eyes and imagine that they live in unusual places such as underwater, in outer space, in a tree, or underground. What would their homes look like? Invite the children to make a group book about their imaginary homes that includes pictures and dictated stories.

Many Houses, Many Homes

Take your children for a walk in your neighborhood. Ask them to look for places where people or animals might live. Search together for houses, apartment buildings, bird nests, barns, ant holes, and other homes. When you return, gather around a sand table, a sandbox, or a basin filled with sand. Show your children props you placed there such as small wooden or plastic houses, people, animals, sticks, rocks, or grass. Encourage a few children at a time to build houses in the sand. Talk together about the various structures your children build. Invite them to tell you about the homes by asking questions such as these: "What kind of home did you build? Who lives there? Would you like to live in a home like that? Why? Why not?"

Straw, Sticks, Bricks, and More

Read or tell your children the story "The Three Little Pigs." Afterward, discuss the building materials the little pigs used. Are the houses in your area made from straw, sticks, or bricks? Or are they made from other materials? Take your children for a walk to discover what materials were used to construct local buildings. Encourage your children to think about why these materials were selected. Lead the children to understand that homes can be built from a variety of materials.

A House to Play With

Make a photocopy of pages 100–101 for each of your children. Provide precut magazine pictures of furnishings for the children to glue in the rooms of the house. (Older children will enjoy drawing the furnishings themselves.) Ask the children to talk about the houses they have made. What are the houses made of? Who lives there?

This Is the House That I Built

Ask your children and their families to save small boxes, cardboard tubes, plastic lids, and other potential building materials. Gather these building materials in your block area and invite the children to use the materials to build houses. They might choose to build houses for people, animals, or make-believe characters. Children can build and dismantle the structures each day. If they are reluctant to tear down a structure, take a photograph to preserve their creation, or provide tape so that they can make their structure permanent. Invite them to paint and decorate the finished structure. Some children might enjoy telling the group a story about who lives in the home or other interesting facts about the building.

Books to Share

Homemade Houses. John Nicholson. Allen & Unwin, 1993. Find out how people from all around the world have used local materials to build houses that suit their particular environment and way of life.

Homes Around the World. Bobbie Kalman. Crabtree Publishing, 1994. Look at various kinds of dwellings, including arctic homes, homes on stilts, homes on boats, and desert homes.

Homes Around the World. Mike Jackson. Illus. by Jenny Mumford. Steck Vaughn, 1995. Take a trip around the world visiting various types of homes from chalets to yurts.

A House Is a House for Me. Mary Ann Hoberman. lllus. by Betty Fraser. Puffin Books, 1978. This rhyming book explains different kinds of homes for animals and things.

Houses and Homes. Ann Morris. Photographs by Ken Heyman. Lothrop, Lee, 1992. Visit houses around the world through fascinating photographs.

Open House Book. Steve Noon. DK Publishing, 1996. Discover the past as you open the doors and peer in the windows of fascinating homes from around the world.

Pictures of Home. Colin Thompson. Simon & Schuster, 1993. This illustrated collection of quotations by children explores the meaning of home.

This Is My House. Arthur Dorros. Scholastic, 1992. Text and illustrations depict the different types of houses lived in by children all over the world.

Little Red Bear

Use the pattern on page 101 as a guide for cutting five bear shapes and five house shapes from five different colors of felt. Use the pieces on a flannelboard as you recite the following rhyme. Let each child in turn match a bear to its corresponding home.

Little red bear
Coming down the street,
Skipping along
On his little red feet.

Little red bear
Is afraid to roam.
Can you help him
Find his home?

Additional verses: Little green bear; Little brown bear; Little white bear; Little black bear.

Jean Warren

Where Do We Live?

Sung to: "The Farmer in the Dell"

A squirrel lives in a tree,
  (Form tree shape with hands.)
A snail lives in a shell.
  (Cover fist with opposite hand.)
A bear lives in a cave,
  (Make fist with thumb inside.)
And it suits her very well.

A fish lives in a bowl,
  (Form circle with hands.)
A bird lives in a nest.
  (Cup hands together.)
I live in a house,
  (Make roof above head with arms.)
Because for me that is the best.

Elizabeth McKinnon

Little Red Bear

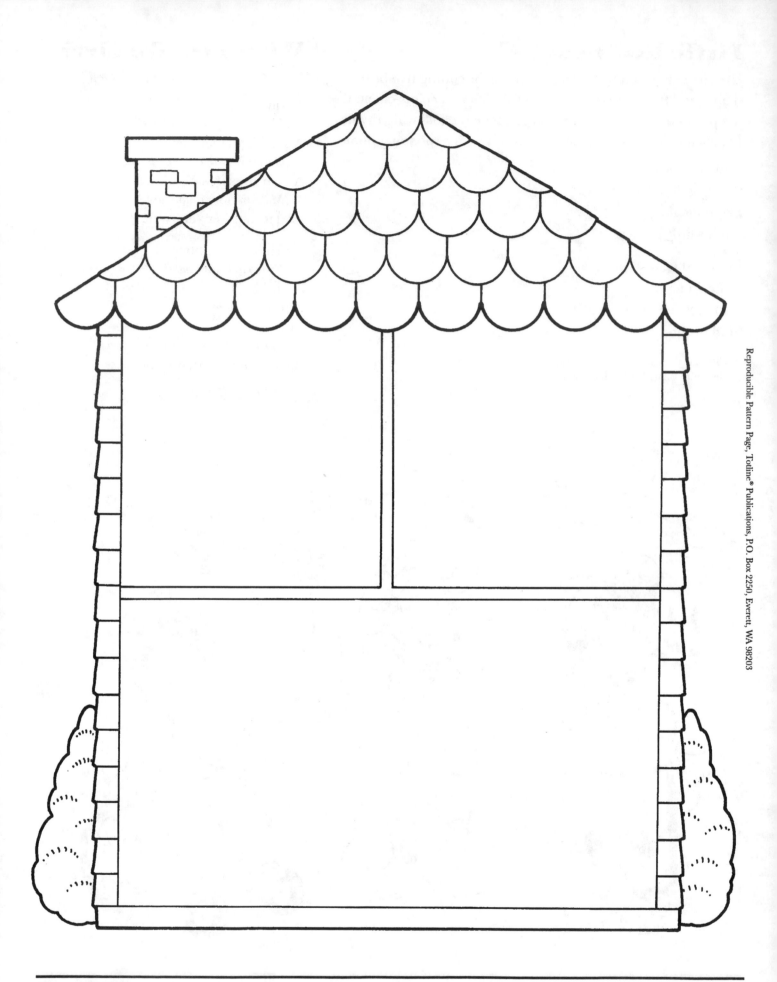

Reproducible Pattern Page, Totline® Publications, P.O. Box 2250, Everett, WA 98203

Keeping Cool

Most children can remember times when the temperature soared. Using "ways to keep cool" as the theme for a learning unit enables children to share and build upon their knowledge. Promote the idea that there are many ways to keep cool. As children share their ideas and experiences, give them opportunities to test and demonstrate them. Let them make fans, spritz themselves with water, or find a shady spot to sit. To involve families in this learning unit, send a note home asking parents to bring in objects they use at home to keep cool, or photos of hot-weather family fun. The following activity is a place to start.

Count the Ways

Ask your children to brainstorm ways of keeping cool on a hot day. Write their ideas on a big sheet of paper and hang the paper where your children can see it. As children think of additional ways over the coming days or weeks, add these ideas to the chart. Have your children illustrate the chart as they wish. Guide your children to recognize that we all keep cool, but do it in many different ways.

The Icebox

Ice has long been an effective way of keeping foods chilled in the hottest weather. Your children may be surprised to learn that long ago, before the invention of the electric refrigerator, people kept their food in iceboxes—insulated cupboards cooled with ice. Today, even though most people have refrigerators in their houses, we still sometimes use ice to chill food for picnics or other times when we cannot be near a refrigerator.

Let your children discover how ice works by making their own icebox. Set out two picnic coolers and have the children fill one with ice and leave the other one empty. Have them put a container of room-temperature juice in each box. Encourage the children to check both coolers and compare the temperature of each. After a few hours, let the children taste the juice from each container. Which juice is cooler?

The Fan Club

Fans are another way of cooling off when the temperature soars. Your children may be surprised to learn that fans may be functional or decorative and that fan-making is an art form. Ask parents and friends to lend fans for your children to examine. Then let your children make fans of their own. Set out white paper plates in assorted sizes; felt tip markers, crayons, stickers, and other decorating materials; craft sticks or tongue depressors; and a stapler. Have the children decorate their plates as desired. Help them staple a craft stick to the bottom rim of the plate to make a handle. When the fans are finished, let your children use them to cool off.

On another day, help your children make fans by folding paper in an accordion shape. Try this with a variety of kinds of paper, such as construction paper, tissue paper, file cards, or newspaper. Which kind of paper works best?

Extension: Have the children sort their fans according to size, shape, or color.

In the Shade

A shady spot can offer protection from the sun's blistering heat. Discuss with your children how sitting in the shade is a way of keeping our bodies cool on a sunny day. Then go on a shade hunt with your children. Ask them to look for shady spots indoors and outside. The next day, let your children take umbrellas outside to create their own shady spots.

Books to Share

Bigmama's. Donald Crews. Greenwillow Books, 1991. Visiting Bigmama's house in the country, young Donald Crews finds the old place and its surroundings just the same as the summer before.

Henry and Mudge in the Green Time. Cynthia Rylant. Illus. by Sucie Stevenson. Macmillan, 1992. For Henry and his big dog Mudge, summer means going on a picnic in the park, taking a bath under the garden house, and going to the top of the big green hill.

Sand and Fog. Jim Brandenburg. Walker & Co., 1994. In this stunning photo-essay about Namibia in Southwest Africa, the color pictures are mysterious and precise, and so are Brandenburg's words about the place and how he took the pictures.

Sand Cake. Frank Asch. Parents' Magazine Press, 1978. Papa Bear uses his culinary skills and a little imagination to concoct a sand cake.

A Summer Day. Douglas Florian. Greenwillow, 1988. The author's brief, rhyming text and crayon illustrations capture the essence of the season and invite shared reading.

This Place Is Dry. Vicki Cobb. Illus. by Barbara Lavallee. Walker, 1989. Survey the living conditions of the people and unusual animals that live in Arizona's Sonora Desert.

Three by the Sea. Edward Marshall. Illus. by James Marshall. Dial, 1981. Three friends relax and tell stories after a picnic lunch.

Watermelon Day. Kathi Appelt. Illus. by Dale Gottlieb. Henry Holt and Co., 1996. Young Jesse waits all summer for her watermelon to ripen.

Cool Card Game

Photocopy two sets of the Keeping Cool cards on pages 106–107. Color the pictures as desired. Glue each sheet to a manila file folder. Cover the pages with clear self-stick paper, then cut the cards out along the solid line. Let your children use these cards for matching and concentration games. To make a Lotto game, make two photocopies of the patterns and prepare them as described above, but cut out only one set of cards. Use the uncut set of cards as a gameboard.

Keeping Cool

Sung to: "Sing a Song of Sixpence"

When the days of summer
Get so very hot,
I begin to look for
A special cool spot.
Sitting by a big fan
Is, oh, so very nice,
Or soaking in a bathtub
Filled with water cold as ice!

Out beneath a shade tree,
That's where I will go—
Drinking lemonade
And dreaming of cool snow.
Maybe I'll make ice pops
Or jump into a pool—
Summer is a lot of fun
If you can keep cool!

Jean Warren

I Can Keep Cool

Sung to: "Mary Had a Little Lamb"

I can keep cool today,
Cool today, cool today.
I can keep cool today.
I will use my fan.

Let your children name some other ways to keep cool.
Sing the song again, substituting their suggestions for *use my fan*.

Jean Warren

Cool Cards

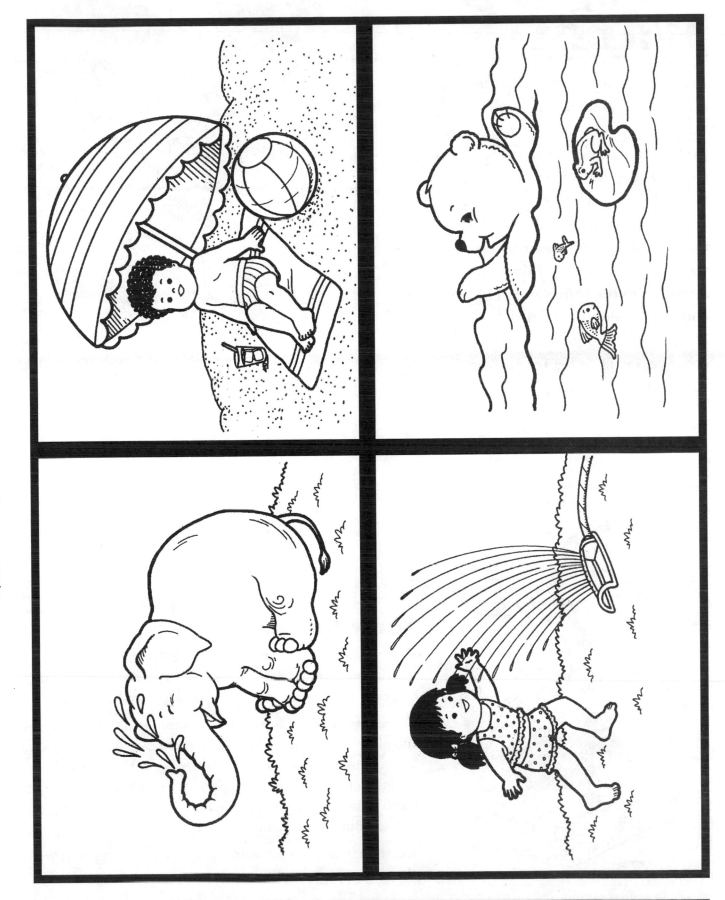

Keeping Warm

People who live in cold climates have many different ways of keeping warm. Some people might enjoy sipping hot soup, while others prefer a steaming cup of tea. Some people wear a hat, while others wrap a scarf around their neck. Some may wear a coat made of wool, while others choose a coat made from animal fur or nylon. As you and your children explore this topic, pay close attention to the things the people in your community do to keep themselves warm. Help your children find out how people in other regions protect themselves from the cold. Remember, there is no right or wrong way—just the warm way.

Snow Blocks

With your children, learn about igloos, the snow houses traditional among Inuit people. Igloos are not permanent homes, but, rather, temporary shelters used when ice fishing.

To make your own igloos, pack snow into empty milk cartons and place them in the freezer. Later, remove the cardboard and let your children see and touch frozen snow blocks like those used to build igloos. (Remind parents to dress their children in warm mittens.) Let your children take these frozen blocks outside and build with them.

Variation: If snow is not available, make ice blocks by filling plastic containers with water and freezing them.

Warm as a Mitten

Supply your children with mitten-shaped pieces of paper and magazine pictures of people and animals keeping warm. (Nature magazines and outerwear catalogs are filled with interesting pictures.) Let the children cut or tear out the pictures and glue them to the mitten-shaped pages. Also provide drawing materials for children who wish to illustrate their pages. Help the children bind their pages between mitten-shaped construction paper or wallpaper covers to make books.

Variation: Cut mitten shapes from discarded sweaters and stitch the edges. Let your children use these to make soft book covers.

Warm Hands

Set out a bowl of snow or ice cubes, mittens made out of construction paper, and cloth mittens (children can use their own). Have your children rub their hands in the bowl of snow or ice until their hands are cold and wet. Then have them place one hand in a paper mitten and the other in a cloth mitten. Which hand warms up more quickly? Which material gets wetter? This activity can lead to discussions about insulation and materials that keep people warm.

Extension: Experiment with mittens made from waxed paper, aluminum foil, newspaper, cotton, and other materials.

Dressing to Keep Warm

Ask parents to donate old clothes for different types of weather. Ask your children to imagine that they are planning a trip to Alaska, where it is very cold. Encourage them to demonstrate which clothes they would pack for their journey.

Variation: If real clothing is not available, cut out pictures of clothing from magazines or catalogs. Ask your children to pick out the clothing people wear to keep warm.

Warmer-Uppers

Cold weather is a time for warm foods and drinks. Why not take this opportunity to explore the many different kinds of foods enjoyed by people who live in cold climates? Invite your children to help prepare and taste warm oatmeal, soup, hot chocolate, hot tea, hot apple cider, spaghetti, or chili.

Variation: Discuss pictures of food and drinks that taste good on a cold day. What are your children's favorite warm foods and drinks?

Warm-Up Cards

Photocopy two sets of the warm-up cards on pages 112–113. Color the pictures as desired. Glue each sheet to a manila file folder. Cover the pages with clear self-stick paper, then cut the cards out along the solid line. Let your children use these cards for matching and concentration games. To make a Lotto game, make two photocopies of the patterns and prepare them as described above, but cut out only one set of cards. Use the uncut set of cards as a gameboard. You can also use the cards along with the "cool cards" on pages 106–107 to explore the contrast between hot and cold.

Books to Share

Frederick. Leo Lionni. Knopf, 1967. In this story, a poet mouse stores up something special for the long, cold winter.

Mama, Do You Love Me? Barbara M. Joosse. Illustrated by Barbara Lavallee. Chronicle, 1991. A child living in the Arctic learns that a mother's love is unconditional.

The Mitten. Jan Brett. Putnam, 1989. Several animals sleep snugly in Nicki's lost mitten until the bear sneezes.

Snow. Nancy Elizabeth Wallace. Western, 1995. Colorful cut-paper illustrations tell the story of a rabbit reminiscing about the first snowfall of the year.

The Snowy Day. Ezra Jack Keats. Viking, 1962. This classic story recounts the adventures of a little boy in the city on a very snowy day.

This Place Is Cold. Vicki Cobb. Illus. by Barbara Lavallee. Walker and Co., 1989. The land, animals, plants, and climate of Alaska are examined in words and pictures. Young children will be fascinated by weather so cold that hair can freeze and break off.

Thomas' Snowsuit. Robert Munsch. Illus. by Michael Martchenko. Annick Press, 1985. Funny things happen when Thomas refuses to wear his new brown snowsuit.

Hot Cross Buns

Hot cross buns,
  (Cross arms over chest.)
Hot cross buns.
  (Pat upper arms with hands, as if keeping warm.)
One a penny,
  (Hold up one finger.)
Two a penny,
  (Hold up two fingers.)
Hot cross buns!
  (Pat arms again.)

Ask your children to name other foods and drinks that taste good on cold days. Repeat the rhyme, substituting the foods your children suggest for *hot cross buns*.

Adapted Traditional

Keeping Warm

Sung to: "The Mulberry Bush"

I can keep my body warm,
Body warm, body warm.
I can keep my body warm
When I wear my coat.

Additional verses: When I drink hot cocoa; When I put on my hat; When I stay inside.

Ask volunteers to name other ways to keep warm. Sing the song again, each time substituting one of their suggestions for *wear my coat*.

Susan Hodges

How I Keep Warm

Sung to: "Hokey-Pokey"

When it's cold outside,
  (Shiver.)
I know just what to do
To keep my fingers warm
  (Wiggle fingers.)
And my head warm, too.
  (Point to head.)
I put on my mittens and I wear my fuzzy hat.
  (Pretend to put on mittens and hat.)
That's how I keep warm.
  (Nod head.)

When it's cold inside,
  (Shiver.)
I know just what to do
To keep my arms all warm
  (Rub arms.)
And my legs warm, too.
  (Point to legs.)
I put on my sweatshirt and I wear my long pants.
  (Pretend to put on sweatshirt and pants.)
That's how I keep warm.
  (Nod head.)

Susan Hodges

Warm-Up Cards

Reproducible Pattern Page; Totline® Publications, P.O. Box 2250, Everett, WA 98203

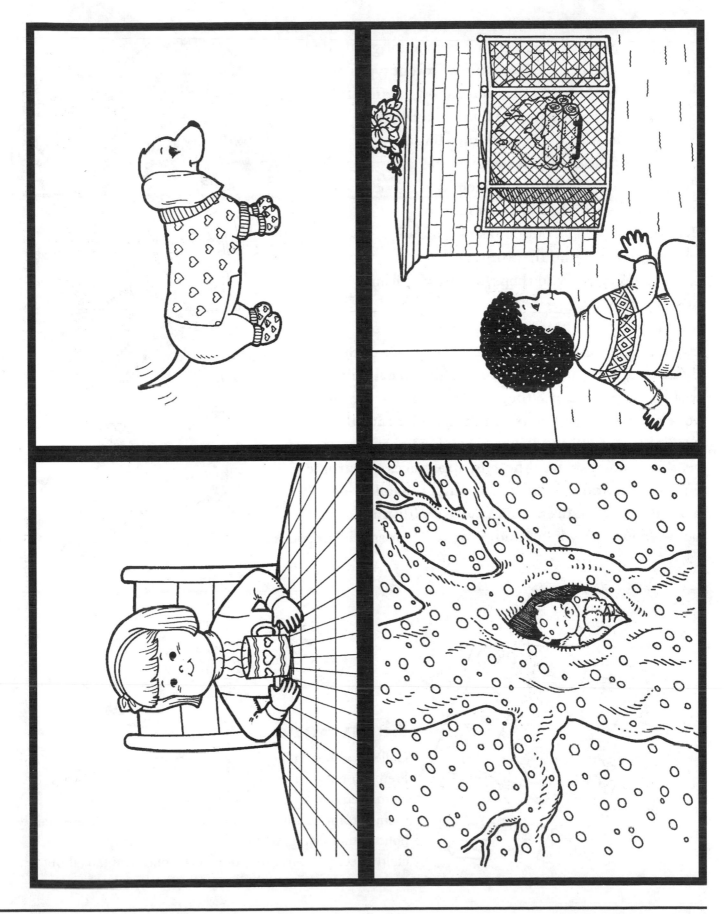

Light

Light is a resource that we usually take for granted, and yet we are exposed to many different types of lights every day. Lights can affect our moods, generate heat, enable us to see, warn us of danger, and give us direction. Almost every culture has a holiday or festival that is dedicated to the celebration of light, in which lights are used in special ways as symbols or decorations. Check out books of holiday celebrations around the world from your local library and read them to your children at storytime.

As you begin this unit, take advantage of opportunities to make your children aware of the lights that surround them. You might take a field trip to a lighting store or a theatrical light shop. Or tour your classroom with your children and locate all of the lights and light switches. Look for lights that are not readily visible, such as those in appliances, electronic equipment, and fish tanks. Through the following activity, your children will explore the distinction between everyday lights and those used for special purposes.

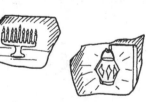

Light Sort

Collect various catalogs and magazines, and have your children tear out pictures of lights and light fixtures. Examine the pictures and talk about how they are alike and different. Help them sort the pictures in two piles, one for lights used mainly at holiday times, and one for lights used everyday. Have each child select a picture from one of the piles and talk about where and when the light might be used.

"Foot-Candles"

Give each of your children taper candles (with wicks cut off) and have them measure various objects in your room. Guide their measuring with questions that make them think about measurement terms. How many candles high is the lunch table? How many candles long is the sandbox? How many candles wide is the chair?

Variation: Collect many different sizes of candles and let your children take turns lining them up from smallest to largest.

Light Board

Create flannelboard cutouts using the patterns on pages 118 and 119, or make your own flannelboard figures by cutting pictures of light from magazines and mounting them on cardboard with felt pieces attached. Ask your children to pretend that the flannelboard is a room, and let them take turns decorating it with lights.

Light Bulb Delight

Light up your children's faces with this simple fruity snack. Cut yellow pears in half lengthwise and place them base side up on a lettuce leaf. Cover the tip with a thick layer of peanut butter or cream cheese, and have your children stick julienne carrot sticks horizontally along the tip as shown, for a screw-in base.

Heat Lamp

Almost every light source generates heat as it gives off light. Illustrate this concept by placing a piece of dark fabric in direct sunlight and another piece directly under a strong desk lamp. Test the fabric after a few hours. Both pieces should be warm to the touch.

Extension: Have each of your children name a light source that gives off heat.

Glitter Bursts

Fireworks are lights that are used around the world for festivals and celebrations. Let your children create fireworks in this art activity. Make a thin paste of 3 parts glue to 1 part water. Give each of your children a small container of multicolored glitter, a straw, and a sheet of paper. Spoon dabs of thinned glue onto the paper and show your children how to use their straws to blow the glue so that it fans out in tendrils. Have them sprinkle glitter on the paper before the glue dries, and let them shake the excess glitter onto a tray. Hang the Glitter Bursts up near a window where the sun will reflect the glittered surface.

Books to Share

Best Friends. Miriam Cohen. Illus. by Lillian Hoban. Collier, 1971. Jim and Paul know they will be best friends when the light goes out in the incubator and they save the baby chicks.

Festivals. Myra Cohn Livingston. Illus. by Leonard Everett Fisher. Holiday House, 1996. From Chinese New Year in January to Kwanzaa in December, poet and artist celebrate the rituals, traditions, symbols, foods, and stories of fourteen multicultural festivals.

Light. Donald Crews. Greenwillow, 1981. The author/artist shows light at night in the city and in the country.

Lights for Gita. Rachna Gilmore. illus. by Alice Priestly. Tilbury House, 1994. Gita a recent immigrant from India, looks forward to celebrating her favorite holiday, Diwali, a festival of lights.

Red Light, Green Light. Margaret Wise Brown. Illus. by Leonard Weisgard. Scholastic, 1994. All day and night the traffic signal blinks its messages of stop and go.

Tonight is Carnaval. Arthur Dorros. Dutton, 1991. A family in South America eagerly prepares for the excitement of Carnaval.

Light Signals

Lights and light signals are often used for safety purposes. Traffic lights help enforce the rules of the road. Signal lights are used to illuminate airport runways. Lighthouses shine high-powered beams out over the water to help sailors navigate their ships at night or in fog. Have each of your children bring a flashlight from home and show them how to turn their flashlights on and off. Dim the lights and let your children have fun making up their own light signals on the walls, floor, and ceiling of your classroom. Encourage your children to practice flashlight safety by instructing them to hold their flashlights in both hands and to shine their lights away from faces and eyes.

Light Talk

What do you think of when you think of lights?
Candles at birthdays, fires on cold nights?
The sun or the moon and the stars in the skies?
The shimmer of fireworks? The flash of fireflies?

Do you think of the lights that you use every day
While you are at home, or outside at play?
Lights on the ceiling and lamps on the ground,
Lights in your toys that blink or twirl around.
Headlights on your bike, on the cars in the street,
Do you have a nightlight that helps you to sleep?

Red lights for stop, and green lights for go,
Why, you meet lights wherever you go.
Lights of all colors, or bulbs of plain white,
Oh, what do you think of when you think of lights?

Carol Gnojewski

Light Switch

Sung to: "Goodnight, Ladies"

We switch the light on,
We switch the light on,
We switch the light on
When it's too dark to see.

We switch the light off,
We switch the light off,
We switch the light off
When it's time to sleep.

We light the candles,
We light the candles,
We light the candles
When it's too dark to see.

We blow out the candles,
We blow out the candles,
Blow out the candles
When it's time to go to sleep.

Have your children act out the motions when you sing the song.

Carol Gnojewski

Electricity

Sung to: "Row, Row, Row Your Boat"

E-lec-tric-i-ty
Is great to have at night.
As soon as it gets really dark
You just switch on the light.

Kathy McCullough

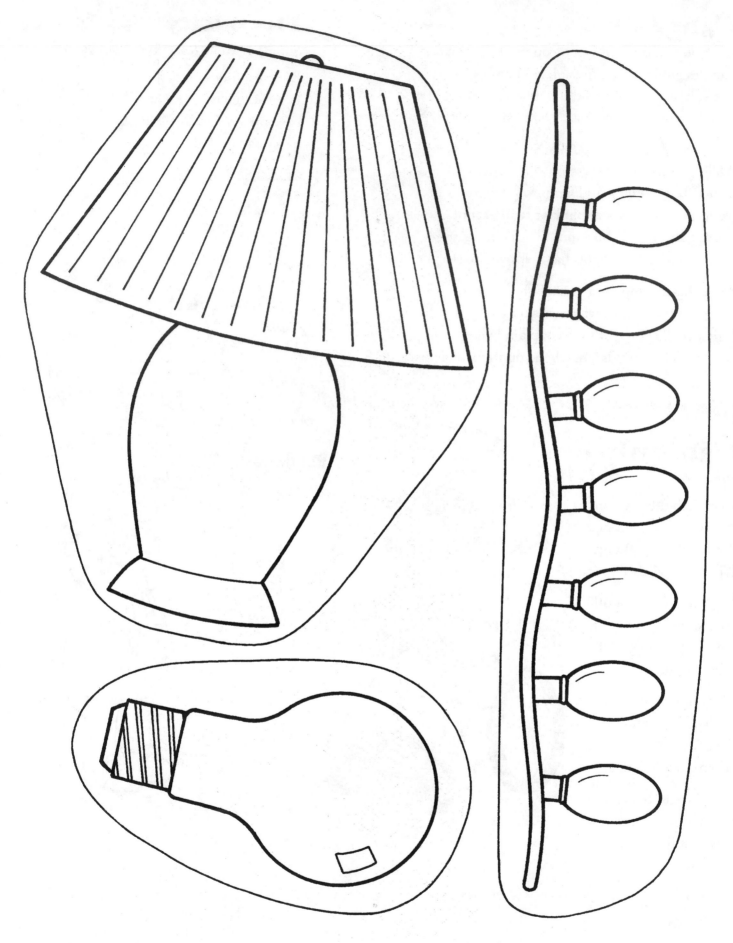

Reproducible Pattern Page, Totline® Publications, P.O Box 2250, Everett, WA 98203

Noodles

An important source of nutrition in many parts of the world, noodles come in many different forms: Italian spaghetti, Japanese udon, and Algerian couscous are just a few. Noodles are also popular with children, and the children in your group are likely to have their own favorite noodle dishes.

Introduce this unit by discussing (and, if possible, sampling) some of your children's favorite ways of eating noodles. Invite parents to share noodle recipes representative of their cultural background. You might even choose to make homemade noodles together. Enjoy!

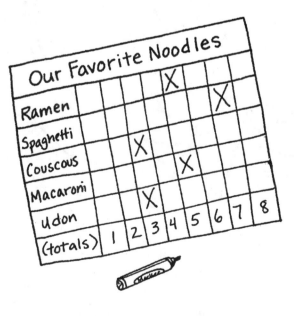

Our Favorite Noodles

On a piece of chart paper, draw an outline for a bar graph as shown in the illustration. Ask your children to name noodle dishes they have tasted. List these in the left-hand column of the graph. Write numerals across the bottom of the graph as shown to indicate totals. Go down the list and name each noodle dish. Ask the children to raise their hands if they like that dish. Together, count how many hands are raised. Record the number on the graph. Together, discuss the results. Guide your children to understand that there are many ways of eating noodles and that we each enjoy noodles in our own way.

As you continue in your exploration of noodles, let your children try each of the dishes listed on the graph. At the conclusion of the unit, make another graph. Have the results changed?

120

Sweet Pastina

Quick-cooking pasta, such as orzo or pastina, is perfect for an exploratory cooking experience. Have your children help you cook the pasta according to package directions. Let them touch the dry pasta, then measure water and pasta for cooking. (Keep children away from hot surfaces.) As the pasta cooks, hold a small hand mirror over the pot. Have your children observe the steamy mirror. What happens as it cools? When the pasta is tender, place it in individual serving bowls to cool. Have your children add raisins and honey to their bowls if desired. Let the children stir and enjoy their warm snack.

It's in the Box

Use boxes of several types of pasta for a sorting game. Place a handful of each pasta in a large bowl. Set aside the remaining pasta for later use. Glue one piece of each to its original box. Challenge your children to sort the pasta in the bowl into the appropriate boxes.

Noodle Maze

Glue dry pasta to shoebox lids to make mazes for your children. Set out small molded animals, marbles, pencil erasers, or other items for your children to move through the maze.

Extension: Once your children become familiar with this activity, let them make mazes for themselves and their friends.

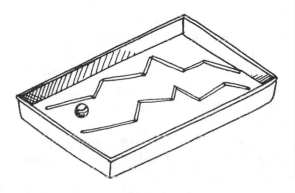

Noodle Game

Purchase pasta in five different shapes. Draw a 5-by-5-inch grid on a piece of posterboard to make a gameboard. Glue a different pasta piece in each box in the left column of the grid. Make as many gameboards as you wish. Combine the remaining pasta in a bowl. To play the game, have one of your children grab a handful of pasta from the bowl and sort it on the grid. Then have the child count the pasta pieces in each row. Which column contains the most? The fewest?

Estimation Jars

Set out two clear jars. Put a few pieces of dry pasta in one jar and many pieces in the other. At the end of the day, ask each child to guess how many pieces are in the first jar, and ask the child's parent to guess how many pieces are in the other one. Offer a sticker or another small reward to each person who guesses. Post the answers the next day. You may wish to play the game for several days.

Shiny Ornaments

Collect a variety of small objects for decorating. Possibilities include cardboard ribbon tubes, plastic-foam balls, cardboard jewelry boxes, and paper cups. Set out bowls of assorted dry pasta. Let each of your children select an object and glue pasta on it until it is completely covered. When the glue is dry, spray the children's projects with metallic spray paint to make festive ornaments. (Use spray paint in a well-ventilated area away from children.) Attach a ribbon, and these ornaments are suitable for hanging.

Books to Share

Cleversticks. Bernard Ashley. Illus. by Derek Brazell. Crown, 1992. Wishing he had something to be clever at like each of the other children in his class, Ling Sung unexpectedly and happily discovers that others admire his prowess with chopsticks.

Daddy Makes the Best Spaghetti. Anna Grossnickle Hines. Clarion, 1986. Making the best spaghetti is only one of Corey's father's talents.

More Spaghetti, I Say. Rita Golden Gelman. Illus. by Mort Gerberg. Scholastic, 1992. Minnie the monkey is too busy eating spaghetti to play with her friend Freddie.

Noodles, A Pop-Up Book. Sarah Weeks. Illus. by David A. Carter. Harper Festival, 1996. This enriched pop-up book shows different types of noodles.

Siggy's Spaghetti Works. Peggy Thomson. Illus. by Gloria Kamen. Tambourine, 1993. Siggy explains how spaghetti is made in the factory and introduces different kinds of pasta.

Strega Nona. Tomie De Paola. Simon & Schuster, 1988. When Strega Nona leaves him alone with her magic pasta pot, Big Anthony is determined to show the townspeople how it works.

Special Treat

Sung to: "Up on the Housetop"

Noodles are a special treat.
Shells and twists are good to eat.
So are spaghetti and bow ties,
Fat or skinny—any size.

Cook the noodles, yum, yum, yummy.
I love noodles in my tummy.
Hand out the forks and now let's eat;
Noodles are a special treat.

Gayle Bittinger

Noodle Shapes

Sung to: "Yankee Doodle"

Noodles come in many shapes.
Some are wiggly, some are straight.
If you taste them, you will see
All noodle shapes taste great!

Ellen Bedford

**Cooking
With Kids**

Noodles with Peanut Sauce

Noodles and peanut butter are a combination most children love. If you cook the noodles ahead of time, this recipe can be prepared without a stove.

    1 package (12 to 16 oz.) elbow macaroni
       Peanut sauce (recipe below)
    1 cup chopped peanuts
    3 cups bean sprouts, washed and dried

To prepare for this cooking experience, cook elbow macaroni according to recipe directions. Toss drained macaroni with peanut sauce in a large bowl. Pour chopped peanuts into a small bowl and bean sprouts into a medium bowl. Set the bowls on a low table and place a ½-cup measuring cup in the bowl of pasta and a teaspoon in the bowl of chopped nuts. Then let the children walk around the table and use the recipe chart on the following page to prepare their serving of noodles and sauce.

Peanut Sauce

    ½ cup creamy natural-style peanut butter
    ½ cup hot water
    3 tsp. soy sauce
    3 tsp. rice vinegar
    1 green onion, thinly sliced
    1 tsp. sugar
    ½ tsp. garlic powder
    ¼ tsp. cayenne pepper (optional)

Combine peanut butter and hot water in small bowl. Stir until smooth. Mix in soy sauce, vinegar, green onion, sugar, garlic powder, and cayenne pepper (if desired).

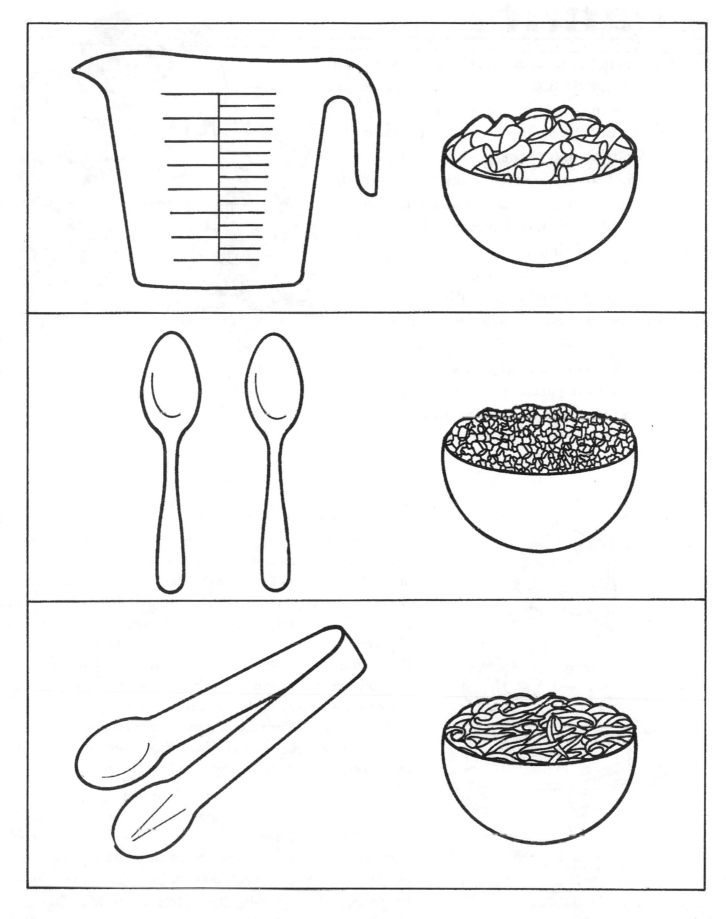

Peanuts

Peanuts are delicious in cookies and candy, ground into peanut butter, or simply roasted. Chances are, your children have tried peanuts in these ways and others. But the peanut is much more than a snack food. Thanks to the work of George Washington Carver, peanuts are used in hundreds of products, ranging from cheese to flour to oil. (Older children will enjoy learning about Carver's accomplishments.)

Explore this fascinating legume with your children through activities that utilize peanuts in many different ways. Provide a generous supply of peanuts in the shell. Use the nuts for cooking and science activities, and the shells in sensory tubs. In the activity below, your children will discover new uses for the versatile peanut.

Invention Fun

Purchase peanuts in the shell. Let your children crack the shells and sort the peanuts into one container and the shells into another. (Use the shells for the activities on the pages that follow.) If a mortar and pestle are available, let your children take turns grinding the nuts into peanut butter. Alternately, seal a handful of peanuts in a resealable freezer bag and add a few drops of oil. Put the bag on a workbench and let your children pound it with a rubber mallet or hammer. (Be sure to use protective eyewear.) They will soon discover that they have made peanut butter. Next, have the children scoop some peanut butter out of the bag and place it on a paper towel. Have them spoon off the butter and notice the stain on the towel. Voila! Peanut oil!

Extension: Set up a snack center with peanut butter, plain yogurt, honey, sliced bananas, granola, and other ingredients. Let your children mix these ingredients to concoct their own snacks. Later, reflect on the day's activities together. Discuss all the ways the peanuts were used. Talk about how each child made his or her snack a little differently, according to his or her own taste.

Peanut Painting

Fill a shallow container with tempera paint and drop in several peanuts in the shell. Cover the peanuts with paint. Have each of your children in turn place a sheet of paper in a rectangular cake pan and spoon one or two paint-covered peanuts into the pan. Have the child tilt the pan to make the peanuts roll, creating a colorful design on the paper.

Five Little Peanuts

Photocopy the patterns on pages 130–131. Color the pictures if you wish and cover the pages with clear self-stick paper for durability. Cut out the peanut shapes and attach a small magnet to the back of each one. Use the pieces on a magnetboard as you read the following rhyme.

Five little peanuts sitting on the floor;
One rolled away and then there were four.
Four little peanuts hiding in a tree;
One fell out and then there were three.
Three little peanuts in a peanut stew;
One was gobbled up and then there were two.
Two little peanuts baking in the sun.
A bird picked one up, and then there was one.
One little peanut was having no fun.
I popped it in my mouth, and then there were none.

Susan Hodges

Find the Peanut

Collect an assortment of small objects, such as a block, a coin, a cotton ball, and a peanut in the shell. Show the objects to your children, then place them in a paper bag. Let your children take turns reaching in the bag and trying to find the peanut by touch.

Books to Share

Nuts to You! Lois Ehlert. Harcourt Brace, 1993. A rascally squirrel has an indoor adventure in a city apartment.

Peanut Butter. Arlene Erlbach. Lerner, 1994. Learn how peanut butter is made, from the cultivation of the peanuts through filling the jars with the nutty spread. Includes simple, no-bake recipes.

Peanut Butter and Jelly. Nadine Bernard Westcott. Dutton, 1987. A simple popular rhyme about that childhood culinary favorite, peanut butter and jelly.

Peanut Butter Cookbook for Kids. Judy Ralph. Illus. by Craig Terlson. Hyperion, 1995. Includes 45 kid-tested recipes with full-color illustrations and easy-to-follow instructions.

Princess Prunelia and the Purple Peanut. Margaret Atwood. Illus. by Maryann Kovalski. Workman, 1995. Prunelia, a proud, prissy princess, plans to marry a pinheaded prince who will pamper her—until a wise old woman's spell puts a purple peanut on the princess's pretty nose.

The Shape of Me and Other Stuff. Dr. Seuss. Random House, 1973. Rhyme and silhouette drawings introduce the shape of bugs, balloons, peanuts, and many other familiar objects.

Sinkers and Floaters

Fill a dishpan with water. Let your children discover what happens when they put shelled peanuts in water. Do they sink or float? What do peanuts in the shell do? How about peanut shells? Later, provide egg carton cups, sponges, and other water props. Challenge the children to find a way to make all of the peanuts float.

The Peanut Plant

Up through the ground the peanut plant grows,
(Crouch down near floor.)

Peeking out its little green nose,
(Slowly start to rise.)

Reaching, reaching for the sky,
(Raise arms above head.)

Growing, growing, growing high.
(Stand on tiptoe.)

Then the flower starts to grow,
(Form circle with arms.)

But it doesn't grow up! Not it! Oh, no!
(Shake head.)

Down it goes, sending shoots underground,
(Bend down and touch floor with fingers.)

And there grow the peanuts, plump and round!
(Kneel and pretend to dig up peanuts.)

Author Unknown

Peanut Butter

Sung to: "Frère Jacques"

Peanut butter, peanut butter;
Fun to chew, fun to chew.
Peanut butter, peanut butter;
Good for you; good for you.

Put the peanuts in a blender.
Add oil too. Add oil too.
Swirl and whirl, swirl and whirl,
Till it's through, till it's through.

Peanut butter, peanut butter;
Now it's done, now it's done.
Making peanut butter;
    making peanut butter—
So much fun; so much fun!

Susan Peters

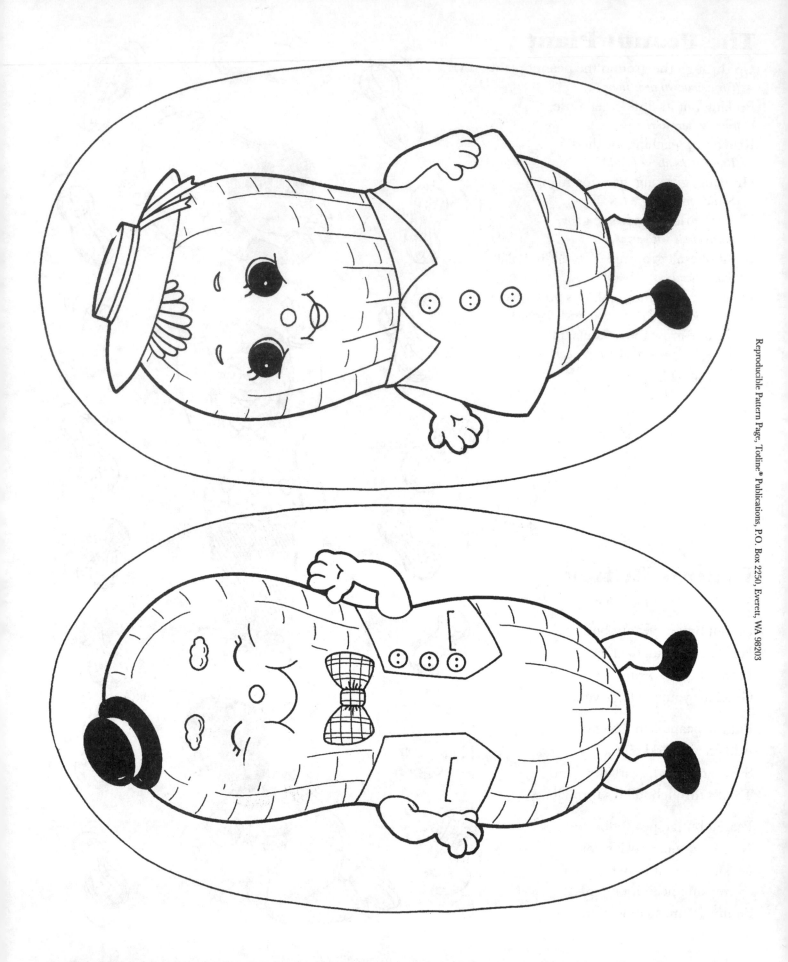

Pets

Pet owners share the pleasure of nurturing another living being. Regardless of its species, a pet requires regular care and attention. By investigating pets, your children can learn more about animals and their care, experience the commitment of pet ownership, and learn new ways of showing love and affection.

Begin by discussing the pets that your children may have at home or visit at friends' homes. What types of animals do people have as pets? Why do people have pets? Also discuss ways that people can show kindness to their pets, such as cleaning, feeding, and exercising them. A field trip to the Humane Society or a visit from a veterinarian will enable your children to find answers to many of their questions. You may wish to culminate this unit with a pet day, in which everyone brings a pet (or a picture of a pet) in for a visit.

Our Pet

Caring for a classroom pet offers young children learning opportunities around the curriculum. If your group has a pet, look for ways to include it in your daily plans. Observing animal behavior is a wonderful science activity, and children are fascinated by what pets eat, where they hide, how they groom themselves, and how they go to the bathroom. Paper shapes of your pet may inspire art projects, group books, and more. Be sure to find books about your kind of pet. Give your children an active role in the care of your classroom animal. Help them generate lists of tasks and safety rules related to the care of your pet. Post the lists where everyone can see them. If your pet needs to see the veterinarian, try to bring your children along. They may notice many similarities between the pet's doctor visits and their own.

A Pet Rock

Your children can create and care for their own pets with this activity. Set out a selection of large smooth rocks and let each child choose one. Have the children paint their rocks with tempera paint. Provide cardboard boxes, soft fabric, and other materials so that the children can make beds for their new pets. What will they name their pets? What do their pets like to do?

Pet Tags

Talk with your children about why it is important for animals that go outside, such as dogs and cats, to have name tags. (If these animals get lost, the owner can be contacted.) Then ask the children to pretend that they are dogs or cats. Have them choose pet names for themselves. Print each child's chosen name on a construction paper tag and let the children decorate their tags as desired. Attach loops of tape rolled sticky side out to the backs of the tags so children can wear them.

Pets Pretend

Seat your children in a circle and choose one child to stand near you. Whisper the name of a type of pet in the child's ear. Ask him or her to stand in the center of the circle and pretend to be that animal without saying its name. Have the other children guess the name of the animal. Continue playing until all children have had an opportunity to be a pet.

Pets or Not?

Discuss with your children the types of animals we keep as pets. Why do some animals make good pets? What animals could you not keep as pets? Why not? Where do these animals live?

Extension: Cut pictures of wild and domestic animals from magazines. Attach each picture to an index card and cover the cards with clear self-stick paper for durability. Have your children use the cards for a learning game, sorting them into two piles: pets and not pets.

Books to Share

Amicio. Byrd Baylor. Illus. by Garth Williams. Macmillan, 1989. Desperately wanting a pet to love, a boy decides to tame a prairie dog who has already decided to tame the boy for his own pet.

I Am the Dog. I Am the Cat. Donald Hall. Illus. by Barry Moser. Dial, 1994. A dog and a cat take turns explaining what is wonderful about being who they are.

I Want a Dog. Dayal Kaur Khalsa. Clarkson N. Potter, Inc., 1987. When her parents refuse to get her a dog, May creates an imaginary dog out of a roller skate.

My New Kitten. Joanna Cole. Photographs by Margaret Miller. Morrow, 1995. Join one very happy girl as she watches her new kitten grow.

My Puppy Is Born. Joanna Cole. Photographs by Margaret Miller. Morrow, 1991. Text and photographs follow a Norfolk terrier puppy from birth to eight weeks later when she goes home with her joyous new owner.

The Outside Dog. Charlotte Pomerantz. Illus. by Jennifer Plecas. HarperCollins, 1993. Marisol, who lives in Puerto Rico, wants a dog very much, but her grandfather will not let her have one, until a skinny mutt wins him over.

The Pets You Love. Jennifer C. Urquhart. National Geographic, 1991. Pictures of birds, dogs, rabbits, goldfish, and other animals with their owners show the reader the responsibilities and pleasures of having a pet.

Whistle for Willie. Ezra Jack Keats. Viking, 1964. A little boy tries to whistle, and when he finally does, his dog Willie comes running.

My Five Pets

Photocopy the patterns on pages 136–137 for your children. Cut out the shapes and attach them to craft sticks or drinking straws to make stick puppets. Make a puppet for each child. Have the children hold their puppets as you recite "My Five Pets" on page 135. As each type of pet is mentioned, have the children holding the corresponding puppets wave them in the air.

My Five Pets

I have five pets I'd like you to meet,
They live with me on my street.

This is my mousie, the smallest of all
He always comes running whenever I call.

This is my kitten, part black and part white.
She loves to sleep on my pillow at night.

This is my goldfish; he swims in his bowl.
He eats and he eats until he is full.

This is my bunny, who hops all around.
She hops high and low, up and down, off the ground.

And this is my puppy, who has lots of fun,
He chases the others and makes them all run!

Adapted Traditional

Strange Little Pet

As I was walking down the street,
A strange little pet I happened to meet.
It had a long _____
And two big _____.
It was covered with _____.
And it walked like a _____.
It liked to eat _____.
And play with my _____.
It made a sound, just like this: _____,
So I took it home and gave it a kiss.

Jean Warren

If You Know a Pet

Sung to: "If You're Happy and You Know It"

If you know a special pet, please stand up.
If you know a special pet, please stand up.
If you know a special pet, if you know a special pet,
If you know a special pet, please stand up.

Additional verses: If you know a special dog, wag your tail; If you know a special cat, purr out loud; If you know a special fish, swim around; If you know a special hamster, wiggle your paws; If you know a special turtle, open your mouth; If you know a special bird, flap your wings; If you know a special rabbit, hop so high; If you love your special pet, please sit down.

Cindy Dingwall

Reproducible Pattern Page, Totline® Publications, P.O. Box 2250, Everett, WA 98203

Reproducible Pattern Page, Totline® Publications, P.O. Box 2250, Everett, WA 98203

Quilts and Blankets

From a thick, heavy quilt to keep the cold at bay to a beautifully woven blanket for ceremonial use, quilts and blankets are an important part of most everyone's life. Quilts are used throughout our homes as colorful wall hangings, decorative furniture covers, safe padding for playpens, and warm coverings on cold nights. Invite each of your children to bring in a special blanket to share with the class. Talk about each blanket individually. What is it made out of? Who made it? Where is it used in the home? Lay all of the blankets out on the floor and point out the different colors, sizes, and patterns. If you have a parent who is a quilter or a weaver, invite him or her in to demonstrate these skills and bring along finished and unfinished work for the children to examine. Most of all, enjoy the wonderful variety of quilts and blankets that your children and their families use every day.

Group Patchwork Quilt

Let your children work together to make their own Group Patchwork Quilt. Give each child a white cloth handkerchief. Have the children decorate their handkerchief squares with fabric paint or fabric markers, and help them write their names on their squares. When the paint or markers have dried, let your children arrange the squares in a square or rectangular shape. Sew the handkerchief squares together. Then place the squares on top of a plain sheet, and cut the sheet to size. Pin the sheet and squares with the right sides together, and sew around three edges. Turn the squares right side out and handstitch the final side closed. Hang the quilt on the wall for your children to admire, keep it in your reading area, or use it in your home life center. Have your children come up with other ideas for its use in your classroom.

Circle Time Space

To create a special space for each of your children at circle time, ask each child to bring in a 2-foot-square piece of old quilt or blanket. Let the children keep their squares in their cubbies. When it is circle time, have the children retrieve their squares and help them arrange the squares into a circle shape.

Variation: Instead of having children bring in their own quilt or blanket squares, let them use ones they make. Give each child a 2-foot square of plain fabric (an old sheet works well) with his or her name written in the middle of it with a fabric crayon. Have the children use fabric crayons to decorate their squares. Following the directions on the box, use an iron to set the wax.

Blanket Fort

Collect blankets and quilts of various kinds and sizes. Let your children use the quilts and blankets to make a fort. Help them drape a large quilt over a table or across two chairs. (A-clamps, found at a hardware store, work well to anchor a quilt on a table or other sturdy piece of furniture.) Have clothespins available for them to clip blankets together. When your children are finished, have them stand back and check out their handiwork—it probably looks like they created their own crazy, patchwork quilt.

Blanket Game

Play this cooperative game with your children. Spread a blanket on the floor. Ask the children to sit on the floor around the edges of the blanket and put their legs underneath it. Have the children raise their legs at the same time to lift the blanket off the floor. How high can they lift it? Can they lower it to the ground all at once?

Books to Share

Eight Hands Round. Ann Whitford Paul. Illus. by Jeanette Winter. HarperCollins, 1991. Introduces letters of the alphabet with names of early American patchwork quilt patterns.

The Keeping Quilt. Patricia Polacco. Simon and Schuster, 1988. A homemade quilt ties together the lives of four generations of an immigrant Jewish family.

Luka's Quilt. Georgia Guback. Greenwillow, 1994. When Luka's grandmother makes a traditional Hawaiian quilt for her, she and Luka disagree over the colors it should include.

The Patchwork Quilt. Valerie Flournoy. Illus. by Jerry Pinkney. Dial, 1984. Using scraps cut from the family's old clothing, Tanya helps her grandmother make a beautiful quilt that tells the story of her family's life.

The Quilt. Ann Jonas. Greenwillow, 1984. A child's new patchwork quilt recalls old memories and provides new adventures at bedtime.

The Quilt Story. Tony Johnston. Illus. by Tomie De Paola. Putnam, 1985. A pioneer mother lovingly stitches a beautiful quilt that warms and comforts her daughter Abigail; many years later another mother mends and patches it for her.

Tar Beach. Faith Ringgold. Crown, 1991. A young girl dreams of flying above her Harlem home, claiming all she sees for herself and her family. Based on the author's quilt painting of the same name.

Ten Little Rabbits. Virginia Grossman. Illus. by Sylvia Long. Chronicle Books, 1991. A counting rhyme with illustrations of rabbits in Native American costumes and blankets, depicting traditional customs such as rain dances, hunting, and smoke signals.

Imagination Station

Animal Blankets

People are not the only ones who use blankets; animals use blankets too. Talk about the various ways blankets are used with animals. A dog or a cat might have a blanket in its bed. A horse wears a blanket under its saddle. Set out several small blankets. Let the children pretend to be animals and their owners. Have the "owners" use the blankets as they care for their "pets."

This Blanket

Sing this song about the various blankets that your children bring in to share.

Sung to: "Mary Had a Little Lamb"

This blanket comes from Katie's family,
Katie's family, Katie's family.
This blanket comes from Katie's family,
It's her teddy bear blanket.

Substitute the children's names for *Katie*. Change the last line to describe each child's particular blanket, for example, *It's red and blue and green* or *It's made from scraps of fabric.*

Gayle Bittinger

The Busy Quilter

I'm a busy quilter,
I sew and sew all day.
And when my quilts are finished,
I can stop and play.

Jean Warren

THIS WEEK...
Mon.: Movie Day
Tues.: Music Day
Wed.: Field Trip
Thurs.: Baking Project
Fri.: Science Experiment

Read!

Blankets Everywhere   *by Susan Hodges*

2

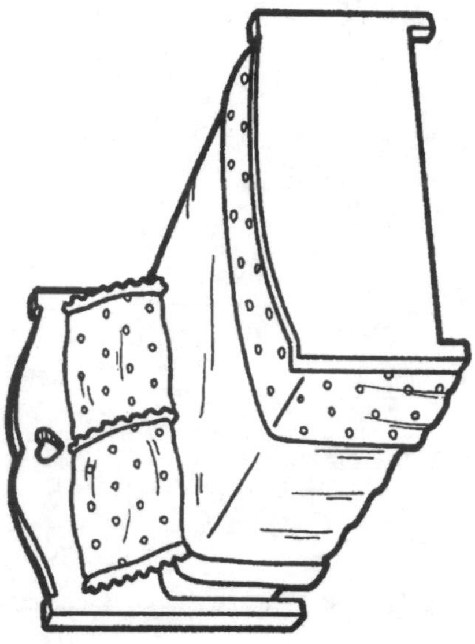

Blankets on the bed.

4

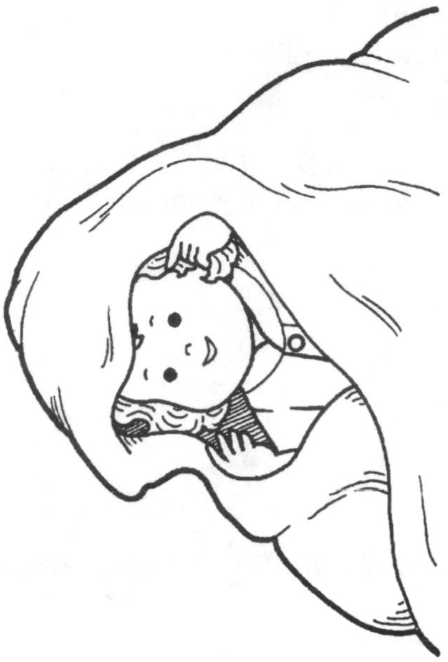

Blankets on my head.

1

Blankets on the baby,

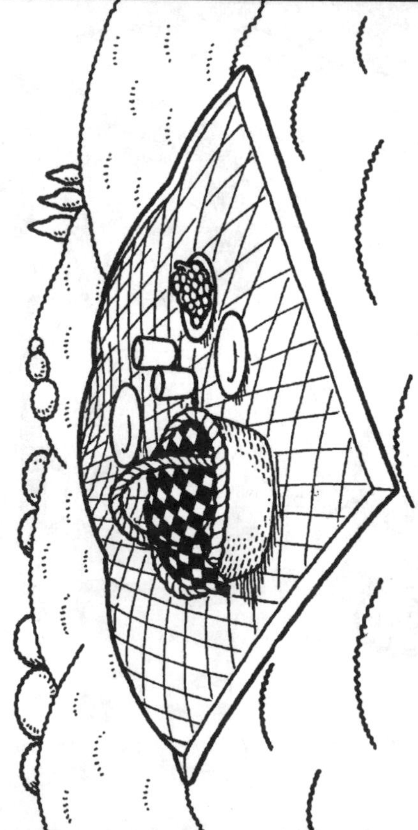

3

Blankets on the grass,

Reproducible Pattern Page, Totline® Publications, P.O. Box 2250, Everett, WA 98203

Photocopy and cut out these pages to make take-home books for your children.

6

Blankets on the chair.

8

Blankets everywhere!

5

Blankets on the horse,

7

Blankets on the floor,

Reproducible Pattern Page, Totline® Publications, P.O. Box 2250, Everett, WA 98203

Rice

Rice is a wonderful teaching prop that can be easily adapted for activities across the curriculum. Nearly half the world population lives partly or almost entirely on a rice diet, and nearly all cultures have special ways of cooking and serving rice for everyday meals and special occasions. Most likely, all of your children will have eaten rice in one form or another. Encourage a rice discussion by having your children name foods they like that have rice in them. Talk about how these foods taste, and what times of the day they are eaten. Try integrating rice throughout your room by placing rice packages in the home life center, substituting rice for sand in sensory tubes and sandboxes, and by using rice for the following art, science, and music activities.

Rice Recipes

There are so many ways to cook and eat rice. Copy the "Rice Recipes" sheet on page 148 and send it home with your children and their parents to complete. Compile all of the recipes in a class cookbook and talk through each recipe with your children. Compare and contrast the various ingredients and cooking methods. Use these recipes at snacktime if convenient.

Rice Paper Mosaics

Rice paper is one of many products made from the rice plant. Let your children explore rice paper in this art project. First make colored rice according to the recipe below. Make several colors of rice, and place them in separate containers when dry. Then give each of your children a piece of rice paper and a squeeze bottle of glue and let them make designs on the paper. Show them how to sprinkle the rice, one color at a time, onto the paper.

Colored Rice

- 1 cup water
- 1 tsp. food coloring
- 1 Tbsp. rubbing alcohol
- 1 cup rice

Combine liquid ingredients in a bowl. Soak rice in the colored water until it is the desired color. Spread colored rice flat on a baking sheet to dry.

Rice Examination

Purchase an assortment of rice and set it out at a discovery table. Provide such accessories as a magnifying glass, a funnel, a sieve, and measuring cups. Let your children discover how the grains differ and how they are the same.

Extension: Photocopy page 149 for your children. Have them glue the corresponding number of rice grains in each bowl.

Stick Together

A special kind of Japanese rice called *glutinous* or *sticky rice* clumps together when cooked. Prepare for the following "sticky" activity by clearing a large space for movement. Then tell your children they are all sticky rice grains and they must work together to form a sticky rice mound. Have them discover different ways to be stuck to each other such as holding hands, hugging, touching backs, and touching stomachs. Work together to move, jump, and sit down as a unit. Sing the following song as you move:

Sung To: "Have You Ever Seen a Lassie?"

The more we stick together,
Together, together,
The more we stick together,
The happier we'll be.

I'll stick to you,
And you'll stick to me,
The more we stick together,
The happier we'll be.

Carol Gnojewski

Rice Shakers

Your children will enjoy making and playing these homemade percussion instruments. Pour uncooked rice into a sandwich bag, and set the bag in the middle of the bottom half of a paper plate. Fold the top half of the plate over the bag and staple the edges of the plate together. Cover the staples with tape. Let your children decorate the outside of their plates with markers, crayons or stickers.

Books to Share

Bamboo Hats and a Rice Cake. Ann Tompert. Illus. by Demi. Crown, 1993. Wishing to have good fortune in the new year, an old man tries to trade his wife's kimono for rice cakes. The Japanese alphabet is incorporated into the text.

Chicken Soup with Rice. Maurice Sendak. Harper & Row, 1962. Celebrate the months of the year while you eat chicken soup with rice.

Everybody Cooks Rice. Norah Dooley. Illus. by Peter J. Thornton. Carolrhoda, 1991. A child is sent to find a younger brother at dinnertime and is introduced to a variety of cultures through encountering the many different ways rice is prepared. Contains nine rice recipes.

The Funny Little Woman. Arlene Mosel. Illus. by Blair Lent. Dutton, 1972. In this Caldecott winner, a little woman in old Japan likes to make rice dumplings.

The Magic Amber: A Korean Legend. Charles Reasoner. Troll Associates, 1994. An elderly rice farmer and his wife are repaid for their kindness and generosity.

The Rajah's Rice. David Barry. Illus. by Donna Perrone. W.H. Freeman, 1994. When Chandra, the official bather of the Rajah's elephants, saves them from serious illness, she exacts from the Rajah a reward more costly than he realizes.

A Tale of Two Rice Birds. Clare Hodgson Meeker. Illus. by Christine Lamb. Sasquatch, 1994. A Thai folktale in which a male and female rice bird die, but meet again when they are reincarnated as a farmer and a princess.

Rice Riddle

I can be long or short or wild.
I can be thrown at a groom and bride.
I can be yellow or white or brown,
I am grown in warm, wet ground.
Smooth as pearl, or starchy and sticky,
I'm best when eaten with chopsticks.
Served with beans I'm mighty nice.
What am I?
You guessed it! Rice.

Carol Gnojewski

I Like Rice

Sung to: "Three Blind Mice"

Rice, rice, rice.
I have rice,
Cooking in a pot,
Cooking in a pot.
Will it be fluffy or gooey or dry?
I never know till it's done and I try
To eat my rice—oh me, oh my,
I like rice.

Carol Gnojewski

Rice Round the Clock

Sung to: "Hush, Little Baby"

Rice in the morning in my cereal bowl.
Rice at dinner in a casserole.
Rice in a pudding is a tasty treat,
But plain white rice is the meal for me.

Carol Gnojewski

Rice Recipes Cookbook

My name: _____

Recipe's name: _____

What you need: _____

_____

_____

_____

_____

How you make it: _____

_____

_____

_____

_____

About this recipe: _____

_____

_____

Reproducible Pattern Page, Totline® Publications, P.O. Box 2250, Everett, WA 98203

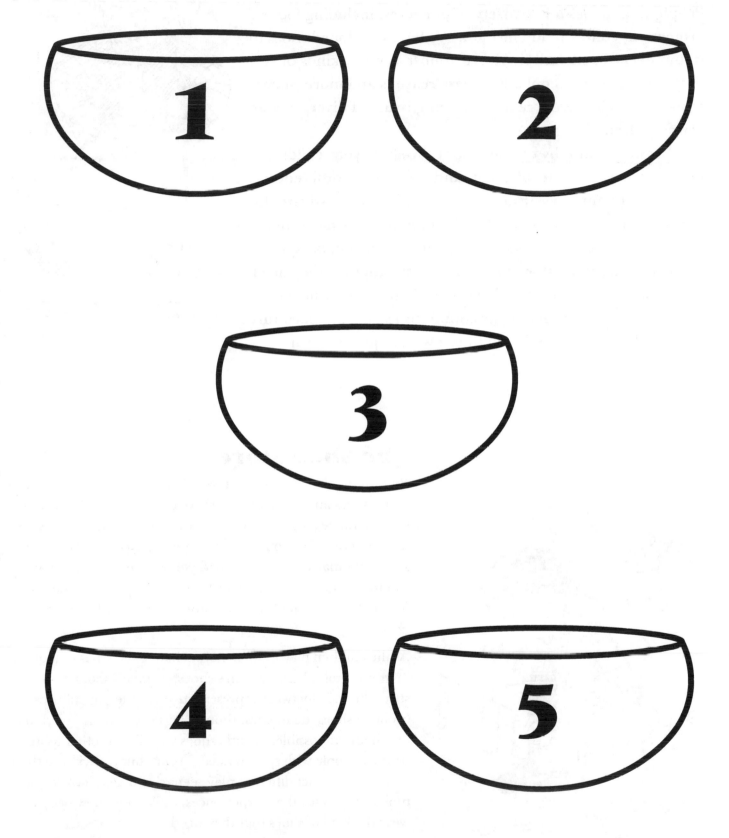

Shoes

People wear shoes for a variety of purposes, including foot protection, comfort, and fashion. We have developed shoes to fit our every need, and there are almost as many kinds of shoes as there are people. For these reasons and more, shoes are a wonderful resource for exploring issues of diversity with your children.

Begin this unit by talking about the shoes your children like to wear. Do they wear different kinds of shoes at different times? Do they sometimes wear no shoes at all? Then investigate the shoes worn in your neighborhood and beyond. Athletes may wear shoes that are specially designed for a particular sport. Dancers wear shoes that give their feet the support they need. Firefighters, construction workers, and others wear heavy shoes for protection. As in our communities, people in cultures the world over have designed their own unique footwear.

The Shoe Store

By running their own shoe store, your children can learn more about shoes and the people who wear them. To set up a shoe store, arrange several chairs in a row. Nearby, stack boxes containing shoes of various sizes, textures, and colors. An actual shoe store may be willing to lend you a shoe sizer. If not, you can make one out of cardboard. Be sure to provide a counter with a "cash register" where customers can pay for their "purchases."

As the children play in their store, change the types of footwear in its inventory. Include men's shoes, women's shoes, and unisex styles. Provide footwear representative of different cultures (wooden shoes, huaraches, thongs) and occupations (work boots, tap shoes). If possible, include shoes with lifts or other footwear used by people with special needs. Your children will use these materials to enact different play scenarios. Later, look for opportunities to discuss their experiences. Talk about how people wear the kind of shoes that they need.

Recycle Old Shoes

Discuss how shoes in a factory all come out looking alike. Give your children an opportunity to turn factory-made shoes into one-of-a-kind fashion shoes. Let them use nontoxic fabric paint, glue, glitter, buttons, rickrack, and other materials to turn old shoes into "designer" shoes. Display the children's creations in their store window.

All Tied Up

To help develop your children's fine motor skills and enhance their understanding of how shoes stay on their feet, encourage them to experiment with an assortment of footwear with different fasteners. Provide oxfords (laces), sandals (buckles), sneakers (Velcro), bedroom slippers (elastic), and boots or skates (hooks and laces).

Share a Shoe Story

During circle time, share the following story opener with your children: "If I were a shoe, what would I do?" You may wish to provide a few shoes from your collection for the children to look at or hold while they think about their verbal responses.

Extension: Write the children's dictated stories on large paper cutouts of different shoes. Older children may wish to "write" their own ideas.

Clomp-Tap-Roll

For imaginative transitions or challenging movement activities, have children pull on make-believe footwear, then "tap dance" to their cubbies, "moon walk" to the snack table, or "skate" to the playground.

Shoes for the Seasons

Use travel posters or ads from travel magazines for seasonal, climatic, or geographical backdrops. After a discussion, encourage your children to select and place actual shoes or magazine cutouts of shoes they might wear next to the appropriate scene. For example, they might place sandals near a poster of a sunny beach, rubber boots next to a rainy street, or ski boots near a snowy slope.

Books to Share

Billy's Boots. Debbie MacKinnon. Dial, 1996. Young children will delight in all they find when they look for Billy's boots.

Cinderella. Barbara Karlin. Illus. by James Marshall. Little Brown, 1989. In her haste to flee the palace before the fairy godmother's magic loses effect, Cinderella leaves behind a glass slipper.

The Country Bunny and the Little Gold Shoes. DuBose Heyward. Houghton Mifflin, 1967. The country bunny attains the exalted position of Easter Bunny and receives a special reward.

The Golden Slipper. Darrell Lum. Illus. by Makiko Nagano. Troll, 1994. At the Red River in Vietnam, a kindhearted girl meets her prince with the help of the animals that she has befriended.

Rosie's Ballet Slippers. Susan Hampshire. Illus. by Maria Teresa Meloni. HarperCollins, 1996. When Rosie's mother buys her a pair of the prettiest ballet slippers she's ever seen, she can't wait for her first lesson.

On Your Feet! Karin Luisa Badt. Children's Press, 1994. Learn about shoes from different eras and from various cultures.

Shoes from Grandpa. Mem Fox. Illus. by Patricia Mullins. In a cumulative rhyme, family members describe the clothes they intend to give Jessie to go with her new shoes.

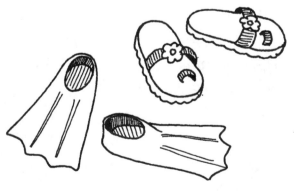

Shoe Charades

Read one of the following rhymes to your children.
Encourage them to imagine what will happen next,
then have the children act out the story they create.

I lost my shoe at the zoo—
Now I don't know what to do!

That bird grabbed my shoe and away he flew—
Where did he go? Can you give me a clue?

Help! My shoe is stuck in the glue!
Can you tell me what to do?

Ellen Bedford

Five Pairs of Shoes

Five pairs of shoes
    (Hold up five fingers.)
In the shoe store.
Someone bought the red ones,
    (Bend down thumb.)
Now there are four.

Four pairs of shoes
For all to see.
Someone bought the blue ones,
    (Bend down pointer finger.)
Now there are three.

Three pairs of shoes,
Shiny and new.
Someone bought the yellow ones,
    (Bend down middle finger.)
Now there are two.

Two pairs of shoes
Standing in the sun.
Someone bought the green ones,
    (Bend down ring finger.)
Now there is one.

One pair of shoes,
Oh, what fun!
Someone bought the black ones,
    (Bend down little finger.)
Now there are none.

Jean Warren

All Kinds of Shoes

There are all kinds of shoes
For all kinds of feet,
To wear at home
Or out on the street.

There are boots for splashing,
And sneakers for dashing.

There are slippers for napping,
And tap shoes for tapping.

There are cowboy boots for riding,
And ice skates for gliding.

But the best shoes of all
Are the ones that fit you
While you're doing the things
You like to do.

Diane Thom

Flannelboard Patterns

Photocopy the patterns on these pages. Cut out the pattern pieces and color them as desired. Cover the pattern pieces with clear self-stick paper and attach a small piece of felt to the back of each one. Use the pieces on a flannelboard as you read the "All Kinds of Shoes" rhyme on page 153 to your children.

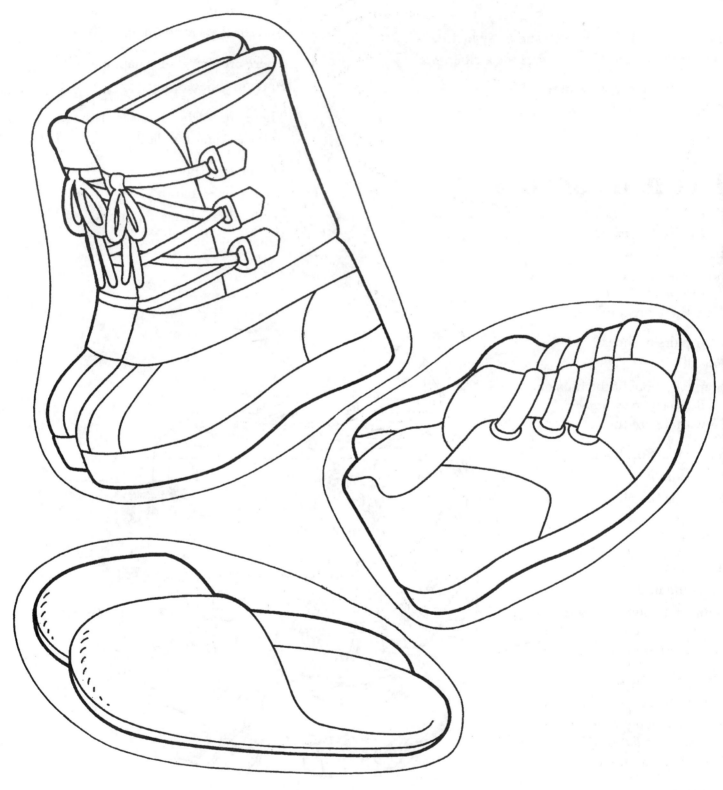

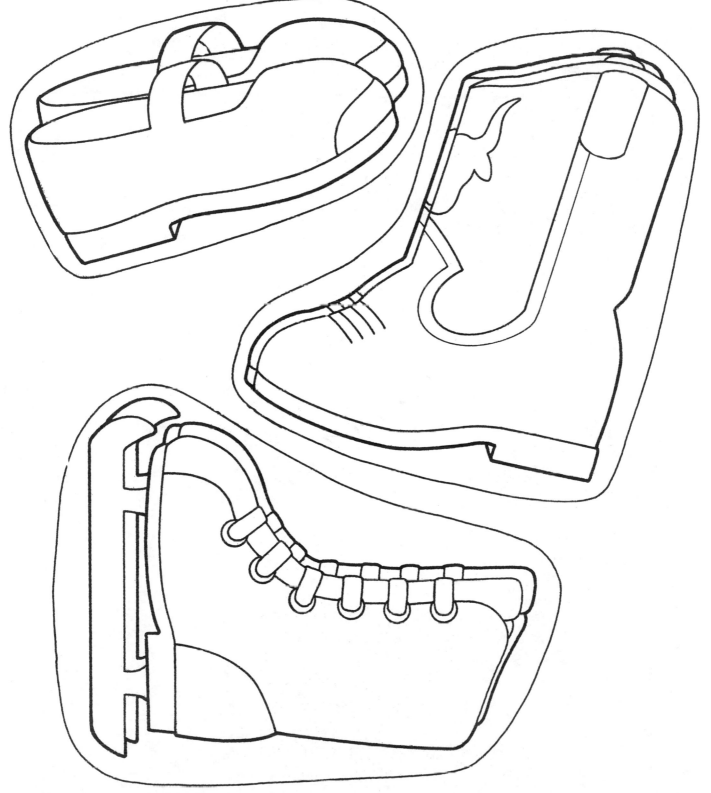

Totline®

PUBLICATIONS

The most trusted name in early learning resources

ACTIVITY BOOKS

BEST OF TOTLINE
Totline Magazine's best ideas.
Best of Totline Newsletter
Best of Totline Parent Flyers

BUSY BEES SERIES
Seasonal ideas for twos and threes.
Busy Bees–Fall
Busy Bees–Winter
Busy Bees–Spring
Busy Bees–Summer

CELEBRATION SERIES
Early learning through celebrations.
Small World Celebrations
Special Day Celebrations
Great Big Holiday
   Celebrations
Celebrating Likes
   and Differences

EXPLORING SERIES
Versatile, hands-on learning.
Exploring Sand
Exploring Water
Exploring Wood

FOUR SEASONS
Active learning through the year.
Four Seasons Art
Four Seasons–Math
Four Seasons–Movement
Four Seasons–Science

GREAT BIG THEMES SERIES
Giant units designed around a theme.
Space • Farm • Zoo • Circus

LEARNING & CARING ABOUT
Teach children about their world.
Our World
Our Selves
Our Town

PIGGYBACK® SONGS
*New songs sung to the tunes of
childhood favorites!*
Piggyback Songs
More Piggyback Songs
Piggyback Songs for
   Infants and Toddlers
Holiday Piggyback Songs
Animal Piggyback Songs
Piggyback Songs for School
Piggyback Songs to Sign
Spanish Piggyback Songs
More Piggyback Songs
   for School

PLAY & LEARN SERIES
Learning through familiar objects.
Play & Learn with Magnets
Play & Learn with
   Rubber Stamps
Play & Learn with Photos
Play & Learn with Stickers
Play & Learn with
   Paper Shapes & Borders

1•2•3 SERIES
Open-ended learning.
1•2•3 Art
1•2•3 Games
1•2•3 Colors
1•2•3 Puppets
1•2•3 Reading & Writing
1•2•3 Rhymes, Stories & Songs
1•2•3 Math
1•2•3 Science
1•2•3 Shapes

THEME-A-SAURUS® SERIES
Classroom-tested, instant themes.
Theme-A-Saurus
Theme-A-Saurus II
Toddler Theme-A-Saurus
Alphabet Theme-A-Saurus
Nursery Rhyme
   Theme-A-Saurus
Storytime Theme-A-Saurus
Multisensory Theme-A-Saurus

PARENT BOOKS

A YEAR OF FUN SERIES
Age-specific books for parenting.
Just for Babies
Just for Ones
Just for Twos
Just for Threes
Just for Fours
Just for Fives

BEGINNING FUN WITH ART
Introduce your child to art fun.
Craft Sticks • Crayons • Felt
Glue • Paint • Paper Shapes
Modeling Dough
Tissue Paper • Scissors
Rubber Stamps • Stickers
Yarn

LEARNING EVERYWHERE
*Discover teaching opportunities
everywhere you go.*
Teaching House
Teaching Trips
Teaching Town

STORYTIME

*Delightful stories with related
activity ideas, snacks, and songs.*

ALPHABET & NUMBER SERIES
Kids Celebrate the Alphabet
Kids Celebrate Numbers

HUFF AND PUFF® SERIES
Huff and Puff's Snowy Day
Huff and Puff
   on Groundhog Day
Huff and Puff's Hat Relay
Huff and Puff's April Showers
Huff and Puff's
   Hawaiian Rainbow
Huff and Puff Go to Camp
Huff and Puff's Fourth of July
Huff and Puff Around
   the World
Huff and Puff Go to School
Huff and Puff on Halloween
Huff and Puff
   on Thanksgiving
Huff and Puff's
   Foggy Christmas

NATURE SERIES
The Bear and the Mountain
Ellie the Evergreen
The Wishing Fish

RESOURCES

BEAR HUGS® SERIES
Encourage positive attitudes.
Remembering the Rules
Staying in Line
Circle Time
Transition Times
Time Out
Saying Goodbye
Meals and Snacks
Nap Time
Cleanup
Fostering Self-Esteem
Being Afraid
Saving the Earth
Being Responsible
Getting Along
Being Healthy
Welcoming Children
Respecting Others
Accepting Change

MIX & MATCH PATTERNS
Simple patterns to save time!
Animal • Everyday
Holiday • Nature

PROBLEM SOLVING SAFARI
Teaching problem solving skills.
Problem Solving—Art
Problem Solving—Blocks
Problem Solving—
   Dramatic Play
Problem Solving—
   Manipulatives
Problem Solving—Outdoors
Problem Solving—Science

101 TIPS FOR DIRECTORS
Valuable tips for busy directors.
Staff and Parent Self-Esteem
Parent Communication
Health and Safety
Marketing Your Center
Resources for You
   and Your Center
Child Development Training

101 TIPS
FOR PRESCHOOL TEACHERS
Valuable tips for teachers.
Creating Theme
   Environments
Encouraging Creativity
Developing Motor Skills
Developing Language Skills
Teaching Basic Concepts
Spicing Up Learning
   Centers

101 TIPS
FOR TODDLER TEACHERS
Valuable tips for teachers.
Classroom Management
Discovery Play
Dramatic Play
Large Motor Play
Small Motor Play
Word Play

1001 SERIES
Super reference books.
1001 Teaching Props
1001 Teaching Tips
1001 Rhymes & Fingerplays

SNACKS SERIES
Nutrition combines with learning.
Super Snacks
Healthy Snacks
Teaching Snacks
Multicultural Snacks

PUZZLES/POSTERS

PUZZLES
Kids Celebrate the Alphabet
Kids Celebrate Numbers
African Adventure
Underwater Adventure
Bear Hugs Health Puzzles
Busy Bees

POSTERS
We Work and Play Together
Bear Hugs Sing-Along
   Health Posters
Busy Bees

Totline® books and resources are available at parent and teacher stores. For the dealer nearest you or a catalog, call 1-800-421-5565

Totline® Books

For parents, teachers, and others who work with young children

TEACHING THEMES

THEME-A-SAURUS®

Classroom-tested, around-the-curriculum activities organized into imaginative units. Great for implementing a child-directed program.

Theme-A-Saurus

Theme-A-Saurus II

Toddler Theme-A-Saurus

Alphabet Theme-A-Saurus

Nursery Rhyme Theme-A-Saurus

Storytime Theme-A-Saurus

BUSY BEES SERIES

Designed for two's and three's— these seasonal books help young children discover the world through their senses. Activity and learning ideas include simple songs, rhymes, snack ideas, movement activities, and art and science projects.

Busy Bees—SPRING

Busy Bees—SUMMER

Busy Bees—FALL

Busy Bees—WINTER

PLAY & LEARN SERIES

This creative, hands-on series explores the versatile play-and-learn opportunities of familiar objects.

Play & Learn with Stickers

Play & Learn with Paper Shapes and Borders

Play & Learn with Magnets

Play & Learn with Rubber Stamps

Play & Learn with Photos

GREAT BIG THEMES

Giant units that explore a specific theme through art, language, learning games, science, movement activities, music, and snack ideas. Includes reproducible theme alphabet cards and patterns.

Space

Farm

Zoo

Circus

CELEBRATIONS SERIES

Easy, practical ideas for celebrating holidays and special days around the world. Plus ideas for making ordinary days special.

Small World Celebrations

Special Day Celebrations

Great Big Holiday Celebrations

EXPLORING SERIES

Encourage exploration with hands-on activities that emphasize all the curriculum areas.

Exploring Sand and the Desert

Exploring Water and the Ocean

Exploring Wood and the Forest

SNACKS SERIES

This series provides easy and educational recipes for healthful, delicious eating and additional opportunities for learning.

Super Snacks

Healthy Snacks

Teaching Snacks

Multicultural Snacks

LANGUAGE

CUT & TELL CUTOUTS

Each cutout folder includes a delightful tale, color figures for turning into manipulatives, and reproducible activity pages.

COLOR RHYMES *Rhymes and activities to teach color concepts.*

Cobbler, Cobbler

Hickety, Pickety

Mary, Mary, Quite Contrary

The Mulberry Bush

The Muffin Man

The Three Little Kittens

NUMBER RHYMES *Emphasize numbers and counting.*

Hickory, Dickory Dock

Humpty Dumpty

1, 2, Buckle My Shoe

Old Mother Hubbard

Rabbit, Rabbit, Carrot Eater

Twinkle, Twinkle, Little Star

NURSERY TALES
Enhance language development with these classic favorites.

The Gingerbread Kid

Henny Penny

The Three Bears

The Three Billy Goats Gruff

Little Red Riding Hood

The Three Little Pigs

The Big, Big Carrot

The Country Mouse and the City Mouse

The Elves & the Shoemaker

The Hare and the Tortoise

The Little Red Hen

Stone Soup

TAKE-HOME RHYME BOOKS SERIES

Make prereading books for young children with these reproducible stories. Great confidence builders!

Alphabet & Number Rhymes

Color, Shape & Season Rhymes

Object Rhymes

Animal Rhymes

MUSIC

PIGGYBACK® SONGS

New songs sung to the tunes of childhood favorites. No music to read! Easy for adults and children to learn. Chorded for guitar or autoharp.

Piggyback Songs

More Piggyback Songs

Piggyback Songs for Infants & Toddlers

Piggyback Songs in Praise of God

Piggyback Songs in Praise of Jesus

Holiday Piggyback Songs

Animal Piggyback Songs

Piggyback Songs for School

Piggyback Songs to Sign

Spanish Piggyback Songs

More Piggyback Songs for School

Totline Books are available at local parent and teacher stores

TEACHING RESOURCES

BEAR HUGS® SERIES

Think you can't make it through another day? Give yourself a Bear Hug! This unique series focuses on positive behavior in young children and how to encourage it on a group and individual level.

Meals and Snacks

Cleanup

Nap Time

Remembering the Rules

Staying in Line

Circle Time

Transition Times

Time Out

Saying Goodbye

Saving the Earth

Getting Along

Fostering Self-Esteem

Being Afraid

Being Responsible

Being Healthy

Welcoming Children

Accepting Change

Respecting Others

1001 SERIES

These super reference books are filled with just the right tip, prop, or poem for your projects.

1001 Teaching Props

1001 Teaching Tips

1001 Rhymes & Fingerplays

THE BEST OF TOTLINE®

A collection of the best ideas from more than a decade's worth of Totline Newsletters. Month-by-month resource guides include instant, hands-on ideas for around-the-curriculum activities. 400 pages

LEARNING & CARING ABOUT SERIES

Developmentally appropriate activities to help children explore, understand, and appreciate the world around them. Includes reproducible parent flyers.

Our World

Our Selves

Our Town

MIX AND MATCH PATTERNS

Simple patterns, each printed in four sizes.

Animal Patterns

Everyday Patterns

Nature Patterns

Holiday Patterns

1•2•3 SERIES

Open-ended, age-appropriate, cooperative, and no-lose experiences for working with preschool children.

1•2•3 Art

1•2•3 Games

1•2•3 Colors

1•2•3 Puppets

1•2•3 Reading & Writing

1•2•3 Rhymes, Stories & Songs

1•2•3 Math

1•2•3 Science

1•2•3 Shapes

101 TIPS FOR DIRECTORS

Great ideas for managing a preschool or daycare! These hassle-free, handy hints help directors juggle the many hats they wear.

Staff and Parent Self-Esteem

Parent Communication

Health and Safety

Marketing Your Center

Resources for You and Your Center

Child Development Training

FOUR SEASONS SERIES

Each book in this delightful series provides fun, hands-on activity ideas for each season of the year.

Four Seasons Movement

Four Seasons Science

PARENTING RESOURCES

A YEAR OF FUN

These age-specific books provide information about how young children are growing and changing and what parents can do to lay a strong foundation for later learning. Calendarlike pages, designed to be displayed, offer developmentally appropriate activity suggestions for each month—plus practical parenting advice!

Just for Babies

Just for One's

Just for Two's

Just for Three's

Just for Four's

Just for Five's

LEARNING EVERYWHERE SERIES

This new series helps parents use everyday opportunities to teach their children. The tools for learning are all around the house and everywhere you go. Easy-to-follow directions show how to combine family fun with learning.

Teaching House

Teaching Town

Teaching Trips

CHILDREN'S STORIES

Totline's children's stories are called Teaching Tales because they are two books in one—a storybook and an activity book with fun ideas to expand upon the themes of the story. Perfect for a variety of ages. Each book is written by Jean Warren.

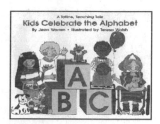

Kids Celebrate the Alphabet

Ellie the Evergreen

The Wishing Fish

The Bear and the Mountain

HUFF AND PUFF® AROUND THE YEAR SERIES

Huff and Puff are two endearing, childlike clouds that will take your children on a new learning adventure each month.

Huff and Puff's Snowy Day

Huff and Puff on Groundhog Day

Huff and Puff's Hat Relay

Huff and Puff's April Showers

Huff and Puff's Hawaiian Rainbow

Huff and Puff Go to Camp

Huff and Puff on Fourth of July

Huff and Puff Around the World

Huff and Puff Go to School

Huff and Puff on Halloween

Huff and Puff on Thanksgiving

Huff and Puff's Foggy Christmas

Totline Books are available at local parent and teacher stores

Active preschool learning— Ideas that work!

Challenge and engage young children with the fresh ideas for active learning in *Totline Magazine.* Developed with busy, early-childhood professionals and parents in mind, these activities need minimal preparation for successful learning fun. Each bimonthly issue is perfect for working with children ages two to six and includes • seasonal learning themes • stories, songs, and rhymes • open-ended art projects and science explorations • reproducible parent pages • ready-made teaching materials • and activities just for toddlers. *Totline Magazine* is the perfect resource for a project-based curriculum in a preschool or at home.

From Totline® Publications